Language—Paradox—Poetics

James J. Y. Liu

# Language—Paradox—Poetics

## A Chinese Perspective

Edited and with
a Foreword
by Richard John Lynn

Princeton University Press
Princeton, New Jersey

**Library of Congress Cataloging-in-Publication Data**

Liu, James J. Y.
Language—paradox—poetics.
Bibliography: p.
Includes index.
1. Chinese language—Versification. 2. Paradox. 3. Poetics. 4. Chinese
poetry—Philosophy. I. Lynn, Richard John. II. Tile.
PL1279.L496   1988   495.1'16   88–6013

ISBN 0-691-06741-4 (alk. paper)

Publication of this book has been aided by a grant from the
Paul Mellon Fund of Princeton University Press

This book has been composed in Linotron Palatino

Clothbound editions of Princeton University Press books
are printed on acid-free paper, and binding materials are
chosen for strength and durability. Paperbacks, although satisfactory
for personal collections, are not usually suitable for library rebinding

Printed in the United States of America by Princeton University Press,
Princeton, New Jersey

# Contents

Editor's Foreword   vii

Introduction   xi

1. The Paradox of Language   3

2. The Metaparadox of Poetics   38

3. The Poetics of Paradox   56

4. The Paradox of Interpretation   94

Afterword: Impersonal Personality   120

Chinese Words and Names   131

Abbreviations   139

Notes   141

Works Cited   157

Index   171

# Editor's Foreword

When Professor James J. Y. Liu suddenly fell ill during the winter of 1985–1986, he had just completed a draft of this book. Although it showed signs of haste in places and would have undergone further polishing by him had his health permitted, it was submitted for publication in its then present form. It gave him great pleasure and satisfaction when Princeton University Press accepted it for publication—this news reaching him just a few weeks before he died in May 1986. In the meantime, he had asked me to do all that was necessary to achieve publication, short of substantial revision of arrangement, translations, arguments, conclusions, and the like, and hoped that I would change things as little as possible. I have tried to carry out these wishes. The book that finally emerged from my editing is still very much his. I limited my contributions to rewriting certain passages for the sake of style or clarity, adding a number of reference notes, rewriting the notes and bibliographical entries for more consistency, adding some transitional phrases, sentences, and short passages where the flow of presentation seems to be too abrupt or disjointed, and making a few corrections of a factual nature. Such transitions and corrections—as well as significantly rewritten passages—are placed in brackets in order to identify them as my work. I also prepared the index and retyped the entire manuscript.

As a scholar and critic Professor Liu had unique gifts. In addition to a very fine intelligence and extraordinary linguistic skills—he seems to have had genuine *tiancai*, "Heaven-endowed talent"—his educational background also provided him with extraordinary opportunities. His schooling in Beijing in the 1930s and early 1940s was a mixture of traditional Chinese classical letters and modern Western-style subjects, including a great deal of English and American literature. His undergraduate education at Fu Jen [Furen] University (the Catholic University of Peking and the only university allowed to stay open in Beijing during the Japanese occupation) offered an exciting cosmopolitan mixture of professors from all over Europe for courses that together covered the major aspects of Western thought and culture—as well as gave Professor Liu the chance to take courses in Chinese literature and history with a number of knowledgeable traditional Chinese scholars and improve his skill at writing essays in classical Chinese. He concentrated in English literature and wrote a B.A. thesis on Virginia Woolf. After the war he entered National Tsing Hua University and began the study of English and French literature—he even had the opportunity of studying with Sir William Empson, who was then at both Tsing Hua and Peking universities. However, after one semester he left for England on a British Council scholarship and continued the rest of his formal education at the University of Bristol and Oxford University. This resulted in an M.A. thesis on Marlowe. He began his varied and brilliant teaching career at the School of Oriental and African Studies, University of London, and later moved on successively to Hong Kong University, New Asia College, University of Hawaii, University of Pittsburgh, University of Chicago, and finally Stanford University, where, except for brief periods of leave, he spent the last nineteen years of his life.

Professor Liu's background and training in Chinese classics and traditional scholarship on the one hand and Western literary studies on the other provided his teaching and writing, in effect, with a double-edged sword: he was a superb philologist and historian of Chinese literature and at the same time a perceptive and erudite critic who had a full working knowledge of modern and contemporary Western methods of literary analysis, interpretation, and evaluation. He had extraordinary control over all the premodern Chinese scholarly sources—bibliographies, encyclopedias, historical sources, individual literary collections, anthologies, and so forth, as well as the vast field of traditional criticism. He could read these materials with great precision and sensitivity—literally and in terms of their local, literary generic, and larger literary and cultural contexts. Since he was truly bilingual, his published translations of both poetry and prose into English are both accurate and fluent, often masterpieces of syntactic equivalence and the *mot juste*.

His approach to criticism kept evolving over the years—beginning with an alignment with I. A. Richards, William Empson, and the New Critics, and shifting later to phenomenologists such as Husserl, Merleau-Ponty, Ingarden, and Dufrenne. Symbolist and postsymbolist poet-critics such as Mallarmé and T. S. Eliot also had considerable influence on him. However, he never merely adopted the views and methods of such Western critics and applied them wholesale to Chinese literature but instead worked out systems of critical theory and practice that synthesized elements from them together with approaches intrinsic to the Chinese tradition, especially those associated with certain figures whom he first called "Intuitionalists" and later "Metaphysical Critics"—such as Yan Yu (ca. 1195–ca. 1245), Wang Shizhen (1634–1711), and Wang Guowei (1877–1927)—critics who in general often viewed literature as a manifestation of the universe, the Dao (Tao), and who were concerned with how writers apprehend the Dao and manifest it in their writings. One can chart the course of his development by reading a succession of his books, all of which are listed among the Works Cited here in this, his last effort: *The Art of Chinese Poetry* (1962), *Chinese*

*Theories of Literature* (1975), and *The Interlingual Critic: Interpreting Chinese Poetry* (1982). The bibliographies in the 1975 and 1982 books and the Works Cited here together contain the great majority of Professor Liu's publications—article-length as well as books—and the interested reader is advised to consult them.

I remember clearly when Professor Liu began to discuss with me some of the issues that were to occupy him for so long: the nature of Chinese poetic expression, how to induce systems of literary theory from the often unsystematic and fragmentary modes of critical discourse in China, how to build on the comparative study of Western and Chinese theories of literature to develop fruitful methods of practical criticism and interpretation—to name but some of them. Our association began during the autumn of 1966 at the University of Chicago. I had the subsequent good fortune to continue this discussion over much of the next twenty years—most of it at Stanford as his student, friend, and sometime colleague. I never expected to become his editor, a task that has proven to be both sad and happy—sad because this book is the last he will ever write, but happy because, in the course of editing, I have had the chance to discuss things with him, in effect, one more time.

In the table of contents to the original draft of this book, Professor Liu indicated that there was to be an Acknowledgment but did not indicate what or whom he wished to acknowledge. Subsequently, I discovered that he had obtained a grant from the Center of East Asian Studies, Stanford University, to cover the cost of typing that manuscript, a task completed by Robert H. Smitheram. I thus acknowledge here this grant and effort.

RICHARD JOHN LYNN

Palo Alto, California

June 1987

# Introduction

The focus of this book is a kind of Chinese poetics that I name "the poetics of paradox" because it espouses the paradoxical view that in poetry, the less is said, the more is meant. Since this poetics originated from a paradoxical view of language seen in early Chinese texts, I deal first with the paradox of language. Instead of proceeding immediately to show how the paradoxical view of language led to the emergence of the poetics of paradox, I consider the nature of all poetics as a metaparadox in chapter 2, before presenting the poetics of paradox in chapter 3. In chapter 4, I discuss the implications of the poetics of paradox for interpretation and the paradoxical nature of interpretation itself. I further suggest possible points of convergence between the traditional Chinese poetics of paradox and contemporary Western poetics and hermeneutics.

Throughout the book I juxtapose Chinese and Western texts without regard for chronology. I do so not in an antihistorical or ahistorical spirit but for the following reasons. First, I am not concerned with claiming chronological priority for Chinese poetics, but with calling attention to a particular kind of Chinese poetics that is intrinsically interesting and that provides points of fruitful comparison with Western poetics. Second, I believe that only by means of juxtapositions of texts from two different traditions can we bring into relief what is truly distinctive in each tradition. Third, such juxta-position will also enable us to become aware of the unspoken presuppositions about the nature of language, poetry, poet-ics, and interpretation that underlie each tradition, thus pav-ing the way for a genuinely comparative poetics, free from both Eurocentrism and Sinocentrism.

Writing in the context of Western literary history, Herbert Lindenberger remarked, "Often, too, the juxtaposition of works or events from widely separated periods can better il-luminate historical constants and differences, continuities and disruptions, than would a chronological narrative."[1] Similarly, the juxtaposition of works from two unrelated cul-tures and in widely different languages can better illuminate cultural similarities and differences than would a chronolog-ical narrative. The similarities may provide a basis for synthe-sis and the differences may suggest new perspectives in which to view familiar problems.

In fact, what I call juxtaposition is similar to what Earl Miner calls alienation. Comparing Japanese and Western conceptions of art, Miner writes, "To deal as it were with prior assumptions of the familiar, one of the most useful pro-cedures is alienation: the bringing to bear on the familiar of what differs but is comparable."[2] However, I have avoided the term "alienation" because, in the first place, with its var-ious Marxian, Freudian, and Brechtian overtones, the term can easily be misunderstood, and second, having grown up in the Chinese cultural tradition but having lived in the West for more than three decades, I do not wish to have the ques-tion raised as to which culture I consider alien. I therefore prefer the neutral term "juxtaposition."

To give one example of unspoken presuppositions under-lying Western and Chinese texts: juxtaposition reveals that, whereas Western critics generally have a mimetic conception of language, Chinese ones influenced by Daoism (Taoism) and Buddhism have what may be called a deictic conception. The former see language as *representing* reality; the latter see it as *pointing to* reality. We shall see some of the consequences of this basic difference in conception of language for poetics.

Although the book as a whole is achronological (rather than synchronic, since I do not treat all texts as if they belonged to the same period), within each chapter the material is presented in chronological order, as far as feasible. Nonetheless, some cross-references to works from different periods are unavoidable.

The book is intended for students of Chinese literature as well as comparatists and others interested in general literary theory, poetics, and hermeneutics. For the convenience of those who can read Chinese, some Chinese characters are given in the text. These, however, are kept to a minimum; the characters for most isolated words, phrases, names, and book titles appear in the list of "Chinese Words and Names" and in the Works Cited.

All translations from Chinese works are mine, but some references to existing translations are given, either in the text or in notes. Throughout I follow the *pinyin* system of romanization.

Language—Paradox—Poetics

# 1

## The Paradox of Language

It should be made clear at the outset that I am concerned with the paradox of language rather than the language of paradox, which Cleanth Brooks identified with the language of poetry.[1] Nor am I concerned with a general survey of Chinese and Western theories of language, for which I have little competence and less inclination. However, I shall touch on such theories as they are relevant to the paradox of language.

The paradox of language may assume one of two basic forms, which may be considered the two sides of the same coin. In the first form, which may be called the obverse side of the coin, paradox arises from the seeming contradiction between the allegation made by many poets, critics, and philosophers, Eastern and Western, in earnest or in feigned despair, that language is inadequate for the expression of ultimate reality, or deepest emotion, or sublime beauty, and the eloquence with which the allegation is made. At any rate, if language is adequate to express the reality about itself, then the allegation cannot be true. Even on the level of everyday discourse, when we say, "Words fail me," we are expressing some kind of feeling, and when we say of something, "It is indescribable," we are giving it a kind of description. In the second form, which may be called the reverse side of the coin, the paradox arises from the seeming contradiction between asserting that ultimate reality, or deepest emotion, or sublime beauty, can be expressed without words, and the very act of making this assertion in words. It was all very well for Śākyamuni to pick a flower and for his disciple Kā-śyapa to smile with instant understanding, without either of them saying a word, but those who recount this legend as an example of wordless communication cannot help using words.[2]

The paradox of language features prominently in early Chinese philosophical texts of the Daoist school (Daojia, not to be confused with Daojiao, the later development of Daoism as an organized religion), especially the *Lao Zi* and the *Zhuang Zi*. Traditionally Lao Zi was said to have been an older contemporary of Confucius (551–479 B.C.); the appellation "Lao Zi" can be taken to mean simply "Old Master," although, according to one tradition, his name was Lao Dan. Another tradition has it that his name was Li Er. Modern scholars have doubted his existence, let alone his authorship of the work attributed to him. Zhuang Zi is identified as Zhuang Zhou, who lived in the fourth century B.C. Both books are probably collections of sayings and parables rather than works by individual authors. However, to avoid the awkwardness of writing "the *Lao Zi* says" or "the *Zhuang Zi* says," I shall sometimes refer to these two works by the names of their putative authors. My references are made to certain ideas and ways of thinking embodied in these works rather than to historical persons. Even when dealing with historically known authors, we need not regard the authors as the causes of the ideas expressed. As Jacques Derrida puts it: "The names of authors or doctrines have here no substantial value. They indicate neither identities nor causes. It would be frivolous to think that 'Descartes,' 'Leibniz,' 'Rousseau,' 'Hegel,' etc. are names of authors of movements or displacements that we thus designate. The indicative value that I attribute to them is first the name of a problem."[3] In a similar fashion I refer to Lao Zi and Zhuang Zi as a way of discussing the problem of the paradox of language.

Not only do the *Lao Zi* and the *Zhuang Zi* contain numerous passages about the paradox of language, but their very existence constitutes an illustration of the paradox, since both deplore, or pretend to deplore, the limitations of language. The familiar words found at the beginning of any traditional edition of the *Lao Zi* assert the inadequacy of language as a means of describing ultimate reality.

> The *dao* that can be *dao*-ed is not the constant Dao;
> The name that can be named is not the constant name.[4]

Most commentators and translators, of whom there are legion, agree that in the first sentence the first and third occurrences of the word *dao* should be taken as "way," and the second occurrence as "speak." An exception among Chinese commentators is Yu Zhengxie (1775–1840), who interpreted all three occurrences as "speak" or "speech." His interpretation has been eloquently repudiated by the eminent contemporary scholar Qian Zhongshu in his monumental work, entitled with ironic modesty, *Guanzhui bian*, which may be freely paraphrased, "Collection of Limited Views."[5]

Among Western scholars, Chad Hansen recently wrote: "The translation of the verbal use of *tao* [*dao*] is simply 'to speak.' Thus a *tao* reflects the features of a discourse or language."[6] He therefore translated the first sentence as "speaking what can be spoken is not invariant speaking."[7] This interpretation is too narrow and does not fit occurrences in many other passages where the Dao is described as the primary force of the universe. My translation attempts to preserve the pun involved (it is hoped that readers will realize that to be "*dao*-ed" is to be dubbed "Dao"). A freer version might say, "The way that can be weighed is not the constant Way," but purists will no doubt prefer the more orthodox rendering—"The way that can be spoken of is not the constant way," as given, for example, by D. C. Lau.[8]

In contrast to Hansen, who thinks that the word *dao* means a total system of names,[9] I think Lao Zi's remark can be interpreted as a denial of the possibility of any linguistic or semiotic system as such. In the terminology of Ferdinand de Saussure, Lao Zi is denying the possibility of language as *langue* but admitting the necessity of language as *parole*, for to call something Dao is a speech act, or an example of *parole*, but to think that this word is part of a constant system, or *langue*, would be a mistake. From Lao Zi's point of view, there could be no structuralist linguistics, which treats language as a closed system of signs. My using the terminology of Saussure, generally considered the founder of modern structuralist linguistics, to suggest that such a linguistics is not feasible is just another paradox.

Despite the assertion that the Dao cannot be named, Lao Zi nevertheless attempts to describe it in various ways and acknowledges the paradox in chapter 25.[10]

> I do not know its name, but force myself to nickname it "Dao,"
> Force myself to name it "great."[11]

While admitting that language is necessary as a makeshift, Lao Zi also warns us that words are not permanent embodiments of reality. His thought here is comparable to Martin Heidegger's crossing out of "Being" (*Sein*) or Jacques Derrida's putting words under erasure (*sous rature*): all three struggle to name the unnameable and implicitly accept the paradox of language in its first basic form.[12]

A variation of the paradox appears in chapter 56.

> One who knows does not speak;
> One who speaks does not know.[13]

This couplet reminds one of the paradox presented by Epimenides (sixth century B.C.), the Cretan who declared, "All Cretans are liars."[14] [This so-called liar paradox is an early example of logical paradox of the type "this statement is false."] As might be expected, some asked why, if this were so, did Lao Zi himself write anything, as the poet Bai Juyi [or

Bo Juyi] (772–846) did in his quatrain "On Reading the *Lao Zi*."

> "One who speaks does not know; one who knows is silent":
> This remark I have heard from the Old Master.
> If you say the Old Master was one who knew,
> Wherefore did he himself write his "Five Thousand Words"?[15]

It is possible that Bai wrote this poem as a *jeu d'esprit* rather than as a serious refutation of Lao Zi, as Qian Zhongshu appears to take it. Qian takes Bai to task for failing to remember certain passages in the *Zhuang Zi* as well as various Buddhist sutras, all of which could have afforded ways out of the dilemma.[16] Perhaps we may enter the spirit of the game and deal with the paradox without resorting to any other text than the *Lao Zi* itself by arguing as follows: since Lao Zi has spoken, he is not one who knows, and therefore his words cannot be taken as true, including the statement "one who speaks does not know," in which case this statement cannot be taken as proof that Lao Zi does not know. This circular argument could go on forever, but for our present purpose we had better stop.

We can avoid the above paradox by adopting Bertrand Russell's distinction between "object language" (i.e. language that talks about things) and "metalanguage" (i.e. language that talks about object language). However, we cannot retroactively prohibit an ancient philosopher from talking about language that talks about language. In any case, to say that "this statement is true of all language except language that talks about language" is to talk about language, and we are back where we started.

Another paradox occurs in chapter 45: "Great eloquence seems inarticulate."[17] In chapter 3, we shall see how this seminal statement greatly influenced the poetics of paradox.

In chapter 78 of the *Lao Zi*, we find what may be called a definition of paradox: "Straight words seem contradictory."[18] Even though this may be a remark added by a later commentator and not part of the original text, as the contemporary scholar Gao Heng believes,[19] it would still represent the Daoist school of thought, which viewed language as a paradox. In fact, some translators have used the word "paradoxical" in translating the above quotation.[20] This term seems to give the game away, however, for a paradox should not call itself such but should seem to be one.

In chapter 81 of the same work, the last chapter according to traditional numbering, appears a variation of the paradox from Chapter 56 that was quoted above.

> True words are not beautiful;
> Beautiful words are not true.[21]

The great critic Liu Xie (ca. 465–ca. 522) in his *magnum opus*, *Wenxin diaolong* (The literary mind: Dragon carvings), tried to explain the paradox away as follows: "Lao Zi disliked artificiality and therefore declared that 'beautiful words are not true'; yet his own 'Five Thousand Words' are refined and subtle, which shows that he did not really reject beauty."[22] Actually, we can deal with this paradox in the same way as we have dealt with the paradox in chapter 56: since Lao Zi's words are beautiful, they cannot be true, including the words "beautiful words are not true," in which case this statement cannot be taken as proof that Lao Zi's words are not true.

Zhuang Zi deals with the paradox of language with even greater subtlety than does Lao Zi. In chapter 2 of the book that bears his name, having remarked (or perhaps paraphrased an existing saying, as A. C. Graham suggested[23] that "the myriad things and I are one," Zhuang Zi then adds: "Since we are already one, how can I say a word? Yet since I have already called it 'one,' how can I say that I have not said a word?"[24] A few sentences later he writes, "The Dao has never had boundaries, and words have never had constancy."[25] He then goes on to say, "The great Dao is not called by name; great eloquence does not speak."[26] The word translated here "eloquence" (*bian*) can also mean "discrimination" (*bian*; the written forms of these two characters were interchangeable) [the former derives from the basic verbal sense of "argue" or "discuss"; the latter, from the verbal sense of "distinguish"]; for this reason A. C. Graham translated the sentence "The greatest discrimination is unspoken."[27] Actually, the two meanings are not mutually exclusive, for to speak eloquently or to dispute is, in effect, to draw distinctions. Since Zhuang Zi in the same chapter advises us not to make distinctions but to take things as they are in their undifferentiated state, he is faced with a dilemma. I consider later how he copes with it.

In chapter 13, Zhuang Zi elaborates on the paradox of language.

> What the world values as speech are books.[28] Books are nothing more than words; words have something that it valued. What is valued in words is meaning; meaning is derived from something.[29] That from which meaning is derived cannot be transmitted in language. Yet the world, because it values language, transmits books. Although the world values them, I shall still think they are not worth valuing, because what the world values is not valuable. Therefore, what can be seen when one looks are forms and colors; what can be heard when one listens are names and sounds. How lamentable that people of the world should think that forms, colors, names, and sounds are adequate to capture the natures of things! If indeed forms, colors, names, and sounds are not adequate to capture their natures, then one who knows does not speak and one who speaks does not know. Yet how could the world know this?[30]

This is of course the same paradox as Lao Zi's, but since the relative dates of these two works are uncertain, we do not know whether Zhuang Zi is echoing Lao Zi or vice versa. All we can affirm is that the presence of identical remarks in both works about the paradoxical nature of language is sufficient evidence that such a view of language was quite influential, if not predominant, in ancient China.

Meanwhile, let us look at Zhuang Zi's famous parable about the wheelwright, which comes immediately after the passage quoted above.

> Duke Huan was reading a book in the hall, and wheelwright Pian was cutting a wheel below. Putting down his mallet and chisel, he asked Duke Huan: "May I ask what words you are reading, sir?"
>
> The Duke replied: "These are the words of the sages."
>
> "Are the sages alive?"
>
> "No, they are dead."
>
> "If so, then what you are reading are the dregs and lees of the ancients."
>
> Duke Huan said: "I am reading here: how dare a wheelwright criticize? If you have an explanation, all right; if not, you shall die."
>
> Wheelwright Pian replied: "I am looking at it on the basis of my own occupation. In cutting a wheel, if you are too slow, it will be 'sweet' and not firm; if you are too fast, it will be 'bitter' and will not go in. Neither too slow nor too fast, what is got by the hand and answered by the mind: that is something that I cannot tell in words, but there is an art in it. I cannot make my son understand it, and my son cannot learn it from me. That is why I am nearly seventy but still cutting wheels in my old age. The ancients and what they could not pass on are dead. So, what you are reading are the dregs and lees of the ancients."[31]

This parable has been told almost ad nauseam throughout the centuries to illustrate that the intuitive mastery of any art cannot be conveyed in words, yet the parable itself is told in words and appears in a book!

The paradox of language in its second form, namely, asserting in words that words are not necessary [to express ultimate reality, sublime beauty, or deepest emotion], appears in chapter 24, where the fictional Confucius [invented by Zhuang Zi] first says, "I have heard wordless words," and then proceeds to describe them in words.[32] In general, words to Zhuang Zi, as they are to Lao Zi, are makeshift devices. We have already seen the remark "the Dao has never had boundaries, and words have never had constancy," and in chapter 25 we read, "The name Dao is what we temporally adopt to make things go."[33] This comment is strikingly similar to what Robert Magliola has said about certain terms used by Derrida: "They are 'provisional names' for the unnameable."[34]

In chapter 26 we encounter another famous parable. "The purpose of the trap lies in the fish: when you get the fish, you forget the trap. The purpose of the snare lies in the hare: when you get the hare, you forget the snare. The purpose of words lies in the meaning: when you get the meaning, you forget the words. How can I get someone who forgets words to have a word with him?[35] We shall have occasion to refer to this parable again, since it has exerted profound influence on Chinese poetics. For the time being, let us simply note the self-conscious paradox in the last sentence.

Not only does Zhuang Zi present the paradox of language, but he also hints at a way of resolving or transcending it, by questioning or even denying certain binary oppositions that are commonly taken for granted. A crucial passage occurs in chapter 2: "Now, is speaking not blowing air? One who speaks says something; it is just what he says has not been fixed. Has he really said something, or has he not said anything? If you think it differs from the twittering of a fledgling, is there really a distinction, or is there no distinction?"[36] In translating the first sentence as a rhetorical question instead of a statement, as previous translators have done, I am following the commentator Ma Qichang (1855–1919), who identified the exclamatory particle *ye* [which occurs at the end of the sentence] with the interrogative particle *ye*.[37] This reading seems more consistent with what follows, for it raises the question whether there is really any distinction between human speech and random, natural sounds, such as the sound of air blowing, just as the last sentence raises the same question with regard to the twittering of a fledgling.

In chapter 25, Zhuang Zi goes further by denying the distinction between speaking and not speaking. "Although his mouth speaks, his mind has never spoken."[38] The point is elaborated at the end of the chapter. "If speech is adequate, then one can speak all day and fully describe the Dao; if speech is not adequate, then one can speak all day and [merely] fully describe things. The ultimate of the Dao and of things cannot be adequately carried either by speech or by silence. Neither to speak nor to be silent is the way to discuss the ultimate."[39]

The refusal to draw a distinction between speaking and not speaking appears in even stronger terms in chapter 27. "If we do not speak, then things will be all the same. Sameness, because of words, becomes differentiated; yet words are the means by which we try to make the differentiated the same again. Therefore, I say: 'No words!' Words are 'no words.' One who speaks all his life has never spoken; one who does not speak all his life has never not-spoken."[40]

The above translation is again based on the interpretation of Ma Qichang, who equated the character *yu* ("and") in the text with *yi* ("because of" or "that by which").[41] Ma's interpretation seems to make much better sense than to take *yu* as "and," for in that case the second sentence would be a strange redundancy: "Sameness and words are not the same; words and sameness are not the same." Even if we take the word *qi* to mean "unity," as Burton Watson did, instead of "sameness" or "same," the sentence would still be redundant, which actually puzzled Watson.[42] Following Ma's interpretation, I would paraphrase the passage as follows: Things in themselves are undifferentiated; only when we speak of them do they become differentiated. Yet when we try to persuade others not to differentiate things, we have no means at our disposal other than words. Zhuang Zi therefore cries out in apparent despair, "No words!" But if "no words" are words (I suspect a sentence *wu yan yan* ["no words are words"] is missing from the text before *yan wu yan* ["words are no words"]), then "words" are the same as "no words." If there is no distinction between the two, between speaking and not speaking, then neither the question whether language is adequate nor the question whether it is necessay would arise any longer, and the paradox of language is thus transcended, or at least bypassed. By rejecting the "either/or" way of thinking and even the "both/and" way of thinking, Zhuang Zi arrives at "neither/nor," which repudiates all binary oppositions and admits all paradoxes. To sum up Zhuang Zi's solution, we may parody Lao Zi's remark "the Dao constantly does nothing but leaves nothing undone"[43] and say, "One constantly says nothing but leaves nothing unsaid [*ren chang wu yan er wu bu yan*]."

In view of the above, I must disagree with Robert Magliola's statements about Daoism in his book, *Derrida on the Mend*, which is mainly concerned with a comparison between Derrida and the Buddhist Nāgārjuna (A.D. ca. 150–ca. 250), although there are occasional references to Daoism. Magliola asserts, "The fact remains that scholars just about everywhere agree that the Tao [Dao] of Taoism [Daoism] has always represented, in one formulation or another, the union of opposites."[44] I do not know who these "scholars just about everywhere" may be, since the only bibliographical reference to Daoism that Magliola provides is to one English translation of the *Lao Zi*, and he makes no mention of Zhuang Zi whatsoever. The quotations from Zhuang Zi given above should be sufficient to show that he did not try to unite or reconcile opposites but actually refused to accept the existence of opposites as such. For similar reasons, I also cannot agree with Magliola that Daoism is typical of the third lemma of the Buddhist tetralemma, which, as explained by him, consists of the following:

1. *X* is *Y*.
2. *X* is not-*Y*
3. *X* is both *Y* and not-*Y*.
4. *X* is neither *Y* nor not-*Y*.[45]

[Since Zhuang Zi rejected both "either/or" *and* "both/and" ways of thinking,] I think that he had already reached the fourth lemma, although he certainly did not elaborate on it as much as the Buddhists did later. However, I do not consider Zhuang Zi to have been a "Chinese Nāgārjuna" or a "pre-Zen [Chan] Buddhist."[46] [The similarities between Zhuang Zi and Nāgārjuna are entirely fortuitous, and the fact that Zhuang Zi had an influence upon the later development of Chan Buddhism in China in no way makes him a proto-Buddhist of any description.]

The paradox of language also appears in another Daoist work, the *Lie Zi*, whose putative author, Lie Yukou, was supposedly a senior contemporary of Zhuang Zi. Modern scholars, however, believe that the work was compiled during the Western Jin era (265–316).[47] The passage involved reads as follows:

> The duke of Bai asked Confucius: "Can one speak subtly with others?" Confucius did not reply. The duke asked, "If one were to throw a stone into water, how would that be?" Confucius said, "A good diver from Wu would be able to retrieve it." "If one were to throw water into water, how would that be?" "Where the rivers Zi and Sheng meet, Yiya [the famous cook] would taste the water and know the difference." The duke of Bai said, "Then indeed one cannot speak subtly with others?" Confucius said: "Why not? But surely with one who knows the wherefore of speech! Now, one who knows the wherefore of speech does not speak with words. Those who fight over fish get wet, and those who chase beasts run, not that they enjoy doing it. Therefore, ultimate speech gets rid of words, and ultimate action is without action."[48]

As commentators have pointed out, the duke of Bai was a grandson of King Ping of Chu (528–516 B.C.) and a son of Prince Jian, who was killed by the state of Zheng. The duke asked the prime minister (*lingyin*) of Chu to attack Zheng, and the latter agreed but failed to carry out his promise. At the time of the above conversation, the duke is planning to kill the prime minister; to "speak subtly with others" pertains to political intrigue. The advice given him by the fictional Confucius is that, no matter how subtle one's words may be, a discerning listener will be able to detect the intent from the subtle hints involved. How this approach to language came to be applied to poetry and poetics will be seen in the next chapter. Meanwhile, we may note that the paradox "ultimate speech gets rid of words" is similar to Lao Zi's paradox "great eloquence seems inarticulate" and Zhuang Zi's "great eloquence does not speak."

The Daoist view of language forms a marked contrast to Western logocentrism, which, as defined by Derrida, is synonymous with phonocentrism or phonologism, namely, the bias in favor of oral speech over writing. This phonocentrism is based on a mimetic concept of language, which accompanies a mimetic concept of art. To Plato and his successors, writing is an imperfect imitation or representation of oral speech, just as art is an imperfect imitation of the phenomenal world, which is in turn an imperfect imitation of the ideal world of perfect forms.[49] Paradoxically, Plato's mistrust of the written word is recorded in writing, and his assertion that "names are in no case stable" [50] coincides with Lao Zi's "the name that can be named is not the constant Name" and Zhuang Zi's "words have never had constancy." In contrast to Western philosophers, Chinese thinkers and writers, including the Daoists, did not have a mimetic concept of language and were therefore free from phonocentrism.

The absence of phonocentrism in Chinese thinking is confirmed by the fact that classical Chinese uses the common word *yan* as a verb ("to speak" or "to say,") or as a noun ("speech, language, word,"), *either spoken or written*. Lao Zi's work, as we have seen, is sometimes called "The Five Thousand Words" (*Wu qian yan*). Chinese writers generally did not differentiate between oral speech and written language, but when they did, they tended to favor the latter. (A few exceptions will be discussed later.) Even illiterate Chinese today have a veneration for the written word, and in traditional China one could see posters with the words *jing xi zi zhi* ("respectfully cherish paper with writing"), exhorting people to put such paper away or burn it, instead of allowing it to be trampled and soiled. This attitude toward the written word may be called graphocentrism, in contrast to phonocentrism.

Graphocentrism can be accounted for by the nature of the Chinese writing system, about which there are still some popular misconceptions in the West. As I explained elsewhere, although traditional Chinese etymology postulates "six scripts" (*liushu*) [i.e. six different principles of graph, or character, formation], two of these concern variant forms and phonetic loans, so that actually there are only four kinds of characters: simple pictograms, simple ideograms, composite ideograms, and composite phonograms.[51] These characters are not arbitrary signs representing what Saussure calls the "sound-images of words," as are the letters of a phonetic script. In the terminology of C. S. Peirce, the simple pictograms are icons, because they resemble their referents.[52] For example, the simple pictogram 日 (ancient form ☉) is an icon for the sun; it is *not* a sign representing the sound of the word *ri* [as this pictogram happens to be pronounced in modern standard Chinese], whose archaic pronunciation has been reconstructed as *niet*.[53] Simple ideograms can be regarded as either icons or indexes, to use Peirce's terms again.[54] The simple ideogram 一 is an icon for the number one, not a sign representing the sound of the word *yi* (archaic pronunciation *iet*),[55] and the simple ideogram 上 (ancient form 二) is an index pointing to "above," not a sign representing the sound of the word *shang* (archaic pronunciation *diang*).[56]

Composite ideograms and composite phonograms are conventional but not arbitrary symbols, for though all arbitrary signs need the sanction of convention to become effective symbols, not all conventional symbols are necessarily arbitrary. Composite ideograms, which consist of combinations of simple ideograms or simple pictograms, are not arbitrary, because the component parts are combined in such a way as to suggest a new meaning. For example, the composite ideogram 好 (ancient form 𢎜) for the word *hao* (archaic pronunciation *xog*),[57] which means "good" or "to be fond of," consists of the simple pictograms for "woman" on the left and "child" on the right. Even composite phonograms are not arbitrary, because the phonetic component [originally a character in its own right] is chosen for its sound, while being dissociated from its own, original meaning. For instance, the composite phonogram 扣 for the word *kou* (archaic pronunciation *k'u*),[58] which means "to strike," consists of the significant [or meaningful] element "hand" on the left and the phonetic *kou* on the right, which is dissociated from its own meaning of "mouth." Thus, composite ideograms and composite phonograms are symbols that, as Peirce might say, "come into being by development out of other signs, particularly from icons, or from mixed signs partaking the nature of icons and symbols."[59]

Western philosophers, with their logocentric bias, have usually regarded Chinese written characters as arbitrary signs. Even Saussure, who recognized that the Chinese writing system is not phonetic, still thought that each written character was a sign that represented a spoken word.[60] This opinion is demonstrably incorrect and also contradicts traditional Chinese views. In the "Commentary on the Appended Phrases" (*Xici zhuan*), one of the commentaries on the *Book of Changes* (*Yi Jing*, or *I Ching*) traditionally attributed to Confucius but probably written and compiled by later Confucians, we read the legend that the mythical sage-king Fuxi (also known as Baoxi) invented the Eight Trigrams, which were later considered the origin of the Chinese script.[61] There and throughout the tradition that follows, these Eight Trigrams are thought to be symbols of the dynamic forces of the cosmos, not signs representing speech sounds.

Another legend is told by the lexicographer Xu Shen (A.D. 30–124) in the postface to his *Shuowen jiezi* (Explanations of simple and composite characters). "Cang Jie, historiographer to [the mythical] Yellow Emperor (Huang Di), invented writing . . . after observing the footprints of birds and beasts."[62] Note that the legend does not say that Cang Jie first invented spoken words and then represented them with written characters [or even that such characters were used to represent words that already existed]. In the early sixth century Liu Xie postulated that human *wen* ("writing" or "literature") is a parallel to natural *wen* ("pattern" or "configuration," such as constellations, geographical formations, patterns on animal skins, etc.), both being manifestations of cosmic Dao.[63]

In general, whereas Western thinkers concerned with the nature of language conceived of writing as a representation of spoken language, which was in turn conceived of as an intermediary between the world and human beings, the Chinese saw a direct relationship between writing and the world, without the necessary intermediacy of spoken language. It is therefore misleading to call Chinese characters logographs or logograms, as some scholars do, apart from the fact that sometimes it requires *two* characters to write one word [i.e. a minimum linguistic free form or smallest independent sense unit], such as *yingwu* ("parrot"), *xishuai* ("cricket"), and *shanhu* ("coral").[64] [Some characters, such as the ones here, *ying*, *wu*, *xi*, etc., are not free "words" and have no independent existence or function in the language.] That Chinese characters do not necessarily represent the sound of spoken words can be further corroborated by the fact that one can understand the meaning of a character without knowing how to pronounce it [in the Chinese language of any time or place, reconstructed ancient or medieval pronunciations, modern standard Chinese or dialects, etc.], as is the case sometimes with Japanese, Korean, and Western scholars of Chinese. [There are, of course, Japanese and Korean "readings" or "pronounciations" of Chinese characters, some of which (e.g. The *on* readings of Japanese) are approximations of once-current Chinese pronunciations. Other pronunciations, such as the *kun* readings of Japanese, however, have nothing whatever to do with *any* Chinese pronunciation. A Japanese seeing the character 山 ("mountain") may at times pronounce it *san* (modern standard Chinese *shan*) when it occurs as part of *some* compound expressions, either borrowed from China during the historical past or actually coined in Japan but still following the principles of Chinese word (*on*) formation—e.g. *sanka* ("mountains and rivers") or Fujisan (Mount Fuji). When it occurs independently with the simple meaning of "mountain," however, a speaker of Japanese will pronounce it *yama*. Here the native Japanese word *yama* ("mountain") is represented by this character, and the mutual identification or association of the word and the character involves meaning only and not pronunciation. The reading *yama* also occurs in certain compound-character expressions, based on Japanese word (*kun*) formation principles—e.g. *yamagoya* ("mountain hut"). However, in either case, a Japanese will understand the character as "mountain," in the same way as a Chinese will.]

The above does not contradict what I wrote years ago in *The Art of Chinese Poetry* against Ernest Fenollosa's and Ezra Pound's misconceptions about Chinese characters.[65] There has been only a shift of emphasis because of changed circumstances: *altri tempi, altri mores*. Then, I was emphasizing that not all Chinese characters are pictographic or ideographic and that most characters contain a phonetic element; now, I am emphasizing that not all Chinese characters contain a phonetic element and that one can understand the meaning of a character without knowing the sound that goes with it. *Pace* Derrida, who spoke of Fenollosa and Pound with apparent approval,[66] I think it is fair to say that they probably sensed intuitively that Chinese characters offered a possible alternative to Western logocentrism, but their interpretations of characters in Chinese poetry owed more to their imaginations than to their knowledge of genuine Chinese etymology. As for Hugh Kenner's defense of Pound's "poetics of error,"[67] I can only reiterate what I have said before: I am concerned not with the effect of Pound's misunderstanding of Chinese poetry on twentieth-century Anglo-American poetry but only with its effects on the English-speaking reader's conception of Chinese poetry.[68] Furthermore, Kenner's remark that "there was no fallacy whatever in [Fenollosa's] understanding of poetry" smacks of ethnocentrism;[69] it assumes that what a modern American critic calls poetry must be a universally recognized phenomenon. Incidentally, Kenner is mistaken in stating that Arthur Waley made a "rhymed" translation of the *Book* (or *Classic*) *of Poetry* (*Shi jing*), and his sarcastic reference to "Professor Waley" is misplaced, because Waley would not even contemplate accepting a chair, declaring that he would sooner be dead! Are these further examples of the "poetics of error"?

Returning to the contrast between Daoism and Western thought we note that, according to Derrida, logocentrism is concomitant with the metaphysics of presence, which, he claims, has dominated the whole Western philosophical tradition from the pre-Socratics to Heidegger. In contrast, the Daoists regard presence (*you*) and absence (*wu*) as mutually complementary rather than diametrically opposed. The words *you* and *wu* are usually translated as "being" or "something" and "nonbeing" or "nothing," but in view of the strong Western philosophical connotations of these English words (one is inevitably reminded of the English translation of the title of Sartre's *L'être et le néant*), I prefer to render these Chinese words "presence" and "absence."

In fact, Lao Zi emphasizes absence more than presence, as can be seen, for instance, in chapter 11.

> Thirty spokes share a hub: where absence is,
>   there the use of the carriage lies.
> Mix clay to make a vessel: where absence is,
>   there the use of the vessel lies.
> Drill holes as doors and windows to make a room: where
>   absence is, there the use of the room lies.[70]

By the same token, Daoism is free from phallocentrism. Lao Zi emphasizes the feminine and seemingly passive rather than the masculine and seemingly active, and whereas Jacques Lacan might identify the "transcendental signifier" with the phallus,[71] Lao Zi appears to identify it with the female sex organ, as in chapter 6.

> The spirit of the valley does not die;
> This is called the mystical female.
> The gateway of the mystical female
> Is called the root of heaven and earth.
> Darkly, darkly, seemingly there:
> Use it, it will not be exhausted.[72]

This orientation is the opposite of phallocentrism and may be called vaginocentrism. In brief, Daoism provides a useful counterweight to Western logocentrism, phallocentrism, and the metaphysics of presence. One can quote from Daoist texts to support Derrida's deconstruction of Western philosophy, or alternatively, one can say that, from a Daoist perspective, such deconstruction is unnecessary.

Several scholars have expressed opinions about logocentrism in relation to Chinese thought that apparently differ from my own. Donald Wesling, in his article "Methodological Implication of the Philosophy of Jacques Derrida for Comparative Literature: The Opposition East-West and Several Other Oppositions," which contains an incisive critique of Derrida, writes, "To say that the representativist conception of writing is linked to the practice of a phonetic-alphabetic writing corresponds not to what we know about Chinese ideograms but to what Ernest Fenollosa and Ezra Pound chose to believe about them.'"[73] He concludes:

> Further correction of specifics in Derrida would involve a demonstration (1) that the Chinese written character has a strong phonetic component which is forgotten or de-emphasized by Fenollosa, Pound, and Derrida; (2) that the Chinese philosophical and literary tradition, for instance in such works as Lu Chi's [Lu Ji (261-303)] *Essay on Literature* [*Wenfu*] and Liu Hsieh's [Liu Xie] *Literary Mind and the Carving of Dragons* [*Wenxin diaolong*], is to the same extent as the Western tradition subject to the myths of origin and presence.[74]

Robert Magliola, in his book *Derrida on the Mend*, asserts baldly that "Taoism in its characteristic form from the beginnings down to contemporary times has been logocentric."[75]

Zhang Longxi, in his article "The *Tao* and the *Logos*: Notes on Derrida's Critique of Logocentrism," points out various Western misconceptions about Chinese writing and proceeds to make, *inter alia*, the following remarks:

> Now the Chinese character *tao* (or *dao*) is a polyseme of which "way" is only one possible meaning. It is very important and especially relevant to our purpose here to note that the word *tao* as used in the *Lao Tzu* [*Lao Zi*] has two meanings: "thinking" (reason) and "speaking" (speech). . . .
>
> . . . at the very beginning of his writing, Lao Tzu emphasizes the inadequacy and even the futility of writing, and does so by playing on the meanings of the *tao*: that the *tao* as thinking denies the *tao* as speaking, yet the two are interlocked in the same word. It is very interesting to note the coincidence—perhaps more than mere coincidence—that *logos* in Greek has exactly the same two meanings of thinking (*Denken*) and speaking (*Sprechen*). . . .
>
> For Zhuang Zi as for Aristotle, words are external and dispensable; they should be cast aside once their meaning, content, or signified has been extracted [with reference to Zhuang Zi's parables about the wheelwright and the fish trap]. . . .

> Logocentrism, therefore, does not inhabit just the Western way of thinking; it constitutes the very way of thinking itself.[76]

I think that some of the disagreements between these scholars and myself may be more apparent than real and that they are due to a confusion in terminology, for which Derrida himself is to blame, for he makes no clear distinction between logocentrism and phonocentrism, although his real target is the latter. To clarify my position, I believe that (1) most Chinese writers are free from phonocentrism, due to the lack of a mimetic conception of writing as a representation of oral speech; (2) even if we take logocentrism in a broader sense to include writing as well as oral speech, the Daoists are still free from this prejudice, since they regard writing and oral speech with equal skepticism and treat both in the same paradoxical fashion; and (3) some other Chinese writers may be accused of logocentrism in the broader sense, or even of graphocentrism, as I suggested above.

As far as Magliola's sweeping generalization about Daoism (Taoism) is concerned, it is supported *only* by Chang Chung-yuan's translation and interpretation of a single passage in the *Lao Zi*, one that probably contains a later interpolation at that.[77] I shall, therefore, advance no new counterarguments here but simply register my disagreement. Let us now proceed to some of the points raised by Wesling and Zhang.

I agree with Wesling that Chinese characters have a phonetic component; I made precisely this point against Fenollosa and Pound more than twenty years ago in *The Art of Chinese Poetry*. I have shifted my emphasis here because I now wish to call attention to the absence of phonocentrism in Chinese thinking about language and writing. As for whether the Chinese conception of writing is mimetic (or representativist, as Wesling calls it), I think one can argue that it is not, despite evidence to the contrary. The legend about Fuxi's invention of the Eight Trigrams, which became the prototype of the Chinese script, does not have a mimetic con-

ception of writing, because, as mentioned before, the trigrams do not represent actual objects but symbolize the dynamic principles underlying the cosmos, and the legend that
Cang Jie invented Chinese characters after observing the
footprints of birds and beasts indicates only that he was inspired by such footprints, not that he invented characters to
represent them. Indeed, if he had done so, the characters
would have had very limited use. [Moreover, we have also
seen above that only a few Chinese characters are pictographic representations of objects; the majority have different and more complex principles (symbolic, ideographic,
phonetic-significant, etc.) of etymology. All such factors argue against a major role for mimesis or representation in the
formation of the Chinese system of writing.]

As for Wesling's other point, I do not dispute the fact that
some Chinese writers may be subject to the myths of presence and origin. In particular, Lu Ji (Lu Chi) was an eclectic
thinker, and Liu Xie (Liu Hsieh), though a devout Buddhist,
adopted a mainly Confucian stance in *The Literary Mind*.[78]
[Both of these figures, at least in part "worldly" Confucians,
seem to have incorporated into their writings on literary art
notions of causality or origin and of the definite, solid "presence" of things, people, events, and the relationships among
them.] However, I still maintain that Lao Zi, Zhuang Zi, and
those strongly influenced by them are relatively free from
these tendencies and, in the main, are not subject to the metaphysics of either presence or "origin" [i.e. a belief in abso-
lutes or an Absolute].

The passages quoted from Zhang Longxi show that there
is considerable agreement between him and myself. He differs in viewing logocentrism as universal and not limited to
Western thinking. This position may be due to a broad understanding of the term. If we take the term in the narrower
sense of phonocentrism, then Zhang may modify his views.
At any rate, as I argued above, even if we accept the broader
sense of the term, it still does not apply to Daoism. Zhang's

comparison of *dao* to *logos* fails to take into account an important difference: in the West, *logos* is identified with God, but Lao Zi took great pains to say that *dao* is *not* the true name of the ultimate. Similarly, Zhang's comparison of Zhuang Zi with Aristotle ignores one vital difference: nowhere does Zhuang Zi suggest [as Aristotle maintained] that he considers oral speech superior to writing. However, Zhang's final conclusion is not very different from mine. "Perhaps this is precisely where the *tao* differs from the *logos*: it hardly needed to wait until the twentieth century for the dismantling of phonetic writing, for the Derridean sleight of hand, the strategy of deconstruction."[79]

Even the Confucians, with their generally positivistic outlook, could not entirely escape from the paradox of language. On one occasion Confucius remarked, "I wish to say nothing." His disciple Zigong then asked, "If you, Master, say nothing, what are we, the younger generation, to pass on?" Confucius replied: "What does Heaven say? The four seasons move on; the myriad things are born. What does Heaven say?"[80] This Confucian concept of a Heaven that says nothing but leaves nothing undone is not very different from the Daoist concept of a Dao that does nothing but leaves nothing undone. The fact that Confucius had to use words to express his wish to say nothing and to explain that words are unnecessary illustrates the paradox of language in its second form. Furthermore, a contemporary description of Confucius as "one who knows it cannot be done but does it,"[81] although it refers to his efforts to reform the world rather than to language, is applicable to anyone who attempts to say the unsayable and may therefore be taken as an acceptance of the paradox of language in its first form.

The same acceptance appears to be present in a statement attributed to Confucius in the "Commentary on the Appended Phrases" to the *Book of Changes*: *shu bu jin yan, yan bu jin yi*,[82] which may be rendered, "Writing does not exhaust words; words do not exhaust meaning." This may sound like an expression of logocentrism and has been taken as such by Zhang Longxi, who translated it "Writing cannot fully convey the speech, and speech cannot fully convey the meaning."[83] However, with the exception of the negative particle *bu*, every word in the statement can be interpreted in more than one way. The word *shu* can mean "writing," "book," or "epistle," or it can refer even to the *Shu Jing* (Book of documents, or Classic of history). The crucial verb *jin* can be taken in a positive sense, "to express exhaustively" or "to describe fully"; or in a negative sense, "to exhaust," "to deplete," "to be exhausted," or "to be depleted"; or in a neutral sense, "to finish" or "to come to an end." The word *yan*, as already noted, can refer to either spoken or written language. The word *yi* can mean "meaning," "idea," "intent," or "sense." Of course, the English word "meaning" can be defined in different ways. If one defines it as that which a speaker or writer intends to express, it is synonymous with "express intent," but if one defines "meaning" as that which a hearer or reader construes from an utterance or a text, then it is closer to "sense," as in "I cannot make sense of it."

Furthermore, it should be mentioned here that, although the word *yi* is not quite the same as "concept" or "universal" or "Platonic form," as Chad Hansen argues, it often did form a third term together with *yan* ("word") or *ming* ("name") and *wu* ("thing") [to provide some of the essential tools of discourse in the writings of various ancient Chinese philosophers]. [Hence, it is an oversimplification and misleading to assert,] as Hansen does, that the ancient Chinese philosophers were concerned *only* with the correspondence between names and things.[84] However, to return to the statement attributed to Confucius, without going through all the possible semantic permutations, some of which would be patently absurd, we may nonetheless consider alternate interpretations. Most scholars take the statement to be an expression of the inadequacy of language, but a recent article by Wang Zhongling argues against this prevailing view. He interprets the statement as follows: "The meaning of *shu bu jin yan* is no more than that books cannot put all words in writing (because of limits of space). Then, the meaning of *yan bu jin yi* is no more than that words cannot speak of all meanings in one's mind (because of limits of time and purpose)."[85]

One might support this interpretation by mentioning that the great historian Sima Qian (145–ca. 90 B.C.), toward the end of a letter he wrote to Ren An, used the expression *shu bu neng jin yi* ("this letter cannot exhaust my meaning").[86] Since then, it has become quite common to end a letter with the expression *shu bu jin yan* ("this letter cannot exhaust my words"), which carries the strong implication, "but you know what I mean." Thus, the statement attributed to Confucius may be interpreted as both a seeming admission of the inadequacy of language and an implicit tribute to the power of language to suggest more meaning than what is explicitly expressed. Interpreted this way, the statement bears comparison with one made by Maurice Merleau-Ponty in his *Phenomenology of Perception*: "Speech is, therefore, that paradoxical operation through which, by using words of a given sense, and already available, we try to follow up an intention which necessarily outstrips, modifies, and itself in the last analysis, stabilizes, the meaning of the words which translate it."[87] This appears to be basically the same idea as that contained in the statement attributed to Confucius, though put the other way round: instead of saying that "words do not exhaust meaning," Merleau-Ponty says that "meaning surpasses words," which may be rendered into Chinese as *yi guo yu yan*.

Let us now consider Mencius (Meng Ke, 372–289 B.C.), regarded as second only to Confucius in the Confucian pantheon. Mencius provides an example of the paradox of language in its first basic form. When his disciple Gongsun Chou asked Mencius what his strong points were, he replied, "I understand words; I am good at nourishing my overflowing *qi*." Then Gongsun Chou asked, "May I ask what is meant by 'the overflowing *qi*'?" Mencius replied, "It is hard to put into words."[88] As if this were not enough of a paradox, Mencius then launched into a long description of the *qi* (variously translated as "breath," "vital force," "spirit," "pneuma," and "ether"), just as Lao Zi described the Dao in various ways after having declared it unnameable. On another occasion, Mencius remarked, "How can I be so fond of disputing? I just cannot help it."[89] This comment is comparable in spirit to Confucius's "knowing it cannot be done but doing it."

Naturally, not all Confucians were sensitive to the paradox of language. Xun Zi (Xun Qing, 340–245 B.C.) developed the doctrine of "rectification of names" (*zhengming*) attributed to Confucius and asserted that names were "conventional" [literally, *ming wu gu yi*, "names have no steadfast/fixed appropriateness"].[90] Since he did not differentiate between oral speech and written language, he apparently failed to notice that not all Chinese written characters were conventional, as we have seen. In any case, the conventionist view of language implies a binary opposition between "nature" and "culture." [I.e. the creation of language is viewed not as something inevitable or *natural* but as part of an accidentally or arbitrarily invented human culture.] However, if we, following Zhuang Zi, refuse to accept binary oppositions, the problem is left unsolved. More specifically, how did linguistic conventions come into being? Xun Zi would have replied, "By order of the former kings." However, history has shown that no king or government or academy can legislate linguistic usage (witness the failure of the French Academy to stop the use of "Franglaise"), and speakers and writers, especially poets, can always invent new words or give new meanings to existing words. Xun Zi's attempt to rectify names or legislate linguistic usage cannot alter the fact that speakers of the same language do not always use words the same way.

One may further ask Xun Zi and latter-day conventionists such as Barbara Herrnstein Smith and Stanley Fish, Who decides on membership of a linguistic community (let alone a literary community), and by what criteria? Consider, for example, contemporary English. Are speakers of "the Queen's English," "Pentagonese," an inner-city dialect, and "Valley Girl talk" all members of the same linguistic community? [Such membership is at best a rule of thumb affair, since it is often so fluid and volatile; the larger "community" consists of so many subgroups, with as many overlapping as mutually exclusive characteristics.]

Among other ancient Chinese philosophers, those who later came to be known as members of the School of Names (*Ming jia*) were especially interested in paradoxes. Their leader, Gongsun Long (third century B.C.) is famous for his paradox *bai ma fei ma* ("a white horse is not a horse"). However, since they were interested in the language of paradox rather than the paradox of language, and since they exerted hardly any influence on poetry or poetics, I shall not discuss them here but refer interested readers to works on them by specialists in Chinese philosophy and linguistics.[91]

A later Confucian who touched on the paradox of language was Yang Xiong (53 B.C.–A.D. 18). He once paraphrased Confucius's statement in the "Commentary on the Appended Phrases," which we examined above, as: "Speech [or words] cannot convey one's heart/mind (*xin*), and writing cannot convey one's speech [or words]. It is hard indeed."[92] This view may sound phonocentric, but Yang immediately goes on to say:

> The sage alone obtained the understanding of speech and the form of writing, letting the white sun shine on them, the great rivers wash them, so that they became vast and irresistible. When words encounter each other as people meet face to face, there is nothing better than speech for drawing forth what one desires in one's innermost heart and communicating people's indignation. As for encompassing and enwrapping the things of the world, recording what is long past to make it clear to the distant future, setting down what the eye could not see in antiquity and trans-

mitting across a thousand *li* what the heart/mind cannot understand, there is nothing better than writing. Therefore, speech is
the voice of the heart/mind, and writing is the picture of the heart/
mind.[93]

Any discrimination here between speech and writing defi-
nitely seems to favor writing. Yang asserts that oral speech
may be adequate for quotidian conversation of casual and
ephemeral interest but that only writing can convey universal
principles across the barriers of time and space.

In another chapter of the same work, Yang approaches the
paradox of language from the hearer's or reader's point of
view instead of the speaker's or writer's. "The sage opened
his mouth freely and formed speech, let go his writing brush
and formed writing. His speech can be heard but cannot be
depleted; his writing can be read but cannot be exhausted."[94]
At first glance this may seem to be a negative statement
about the limits of understanding, but closer scrutiny reveals
that it is really a positive statement about the inexhaustibility
of meaning in the statements of a sage. Thus, instead of giving up reading in despair, one should continue to read in the
hope of discovering ever more meanings that have been hith-
erto unperceived. Similarly, the realization of the limits of
language as a medium of expression should not lead to the
abandonment of all writing but rather encourage one to continue to write in the hope of suggesting ever more unstated
meanings. Seen in this light, Yang Xiong's remarks may be
said to have paved the way for later critics who advocated
"meaning beyond words" or "limited words with unlimited
meaning," ideas that will be explored later in this book.

During the Wei (220–265) and Jin (265–419) periods, the
question whether language can fully express meaning was a
topic of considerable controversy, one that has been revived
by some Chinese scholars in recent years. To pursue all the
details of this controversy would take us too far afield, but it
is possible to obtain an overview of it by seeing how one

writer tried to turn the table (*fan an*) on the saying "words do not exhaust meaning."[95] Ouyang Jian (d. A.D. 300), in his essay "Words Do Exhaust Meaning" (*Yan jin yi lun*), wrote as follows:

> Now, Heaven does not speak, yet the four seasons move on; the sage does not speak, yet his discernment remains. Forms do not wait for names before the square and the circle appear; colors do not wait for designations before black and white are manifest. If so, then names, with regard to things, have no use; words, with regard to principles, can do nothing. Yet both the ancients and the moderns have engaged in the rectification of names, and sages and enlightened men cannot abolish words. Why is this so? It is truly because when principles are obtained in the heart/mind, without words one cannot let the intent flow freely, and when things are fixed by themselves, without words one cannot distinguish them. Without words to let the intent of the heart/mind flow freely, there would be no means by which we could contact each other; without names to distinguish things, our discernment would not be manifest. When discernment is manifest, then names and categories differ; when words and designations come into contact with each other, then one's feelings and intents flow freely. When we trace their origins and seek their roots, we find that it is not that things have their natural names or that principles have their inevitable designations. If we wish to distinguish things, then we must differentiate their names; if we wish to declare our intents, then we must establish their designations. Names shift, according to things; words change, according to principles. This is just like an echo responding to the issuance of a sound, or a shadow attaching itself to the existence of a body: one cannot separate them into two. If they [words and meanings] cannot be separated into two, then there is no word that does not exhaust the meaning.[96]

The essay assumes the form of a debate, or rather pseudo-debate. Ouyang first plays the devil's advocate and argues for the proposition that language is not necessary, then proceeds to argue for the counterproposition that language is necessary, and finally reaches a conclusion. His arguments, counterarguments, and conclusion may be summarized as follows:

1. Language is not necessary.
   A. Heaven does not speak, yet accomplishes natural transformations.
   B. Sages discern the natures of things without having to speak.
   C. Things exist independently of words.
2. Language is necessary.
   A. Without words we would not be able to express our intents and so would not be able to communicate with each other.
   B. Without words we would not be able to differentiate things or discern their natures.
   C. Things have no natural names; we need words to name them.
3. Conclusion: Names and things are inseparable; words and meanings are inseparable. Therefore, words do exhaust meanings.

Ingenious as he may be, Ouyang raises more problems than he solves. In the first place, the assertion that things exist independently of words (argument 1C) and the assertion that things have no natural names (2C) contradict the conclusion that names and things are inseparable. Second, with regard to argument 2C, it is not clear how names are attached to things. Ouyang appears to be following Xun Zi, for he also fails to differentiate between oral speech and written language, with its inherent problems. Third, Ouyang does not make it clear whether he considers the relationship between *ming* ("name") and *wu* ("thing") to be parallel to, or identical with, that between *yan* ("word") and *yi* ("meaning"), the last of which he apparently uses as a synonym for *zhi* ("intent"). If we assume that "name" and "word" are synonymous, can we also assume that "thing" and "meaning" are synonymous? If not, what is the relationship between them? The confusion shows that Ouyang did not perceive a tripartite relationship among "word," "meaning," and "thing" (or, in the terminology of modern linguistics, "signifier," "signified," and "referent"), as did his contemporary Lu Ji, whose views we shall discuss in the next chapter.

Finally, the debate here is conducted on two levels. The arguments in favor of the proposition that language is unnecessary pertain to the level of ultimate reality, whereas those in favor of the counterproposition pertain to the level of everyday discourse. The latter, therefore, do not necessarily invalidate the former. For the same reason, the essay does not necessarily invalidate the saying "words do not exhaust meaning," which pertains to the level of ultimate reality. Although the debate bears some resemblance to Hegel's dialectic, the conclusion cannot be called a successful synthesis of the thesis and antithesis. In fact, Ouyang's arguments do not go beyond Lao Zi's remark, "The name that can be named is not the constant Name," or Zhuang Zi's remark, "Words have never had constancy."[97]

It should be evident from the quotations and discussions above that early Chinese texts, especially Daoist ones, provided sufficient ground for a poetics of paradox to emerge, without further impetus. However, such impetus was in fact supplied by Buddhism, which was first introduced into China in the first century A.D. but did not become widely popular until the fifth century. Buddhism illustrates the paradox of language on a mind-boggling scale. We have already encountered the legend about Śākyamuni's wordless communication with his disciple Kāśyapa, which illustrates the paradox of language in its second basic form. The paradox in its first basic form is illustrated by the fact that, although the Buddhists claim that ultimate reality cannot be conveyed in words, they have produced more scriptures and commentaries than have the followers of any other religion. Some Buddhists, such as Sengzhao (384–414), tried to explain the paradox with the "theory of twofold truth": ultimate truth or true meaning (*zhen di*, the Chinese translation of *paramārtha-*

*satya*) and worldly truth or secular meaning (*su di*, the translation of *saṁvṛti-satya*).[98] The monk Huijiao (497–554) applied this theory when he wrote: "The sage . . . borrowed subtle words to make a ford to the Way, and relied on images to communicate the truth. Therefore, it is said: 'Arms are inauspicious instruments, and the sage uses them when he cannot help it. Words are not true things; the sage puts them forth when he cannot help it.' "[99]

This quotation, which is partly borrowed from the *Lao Zi*, provides a justification for Buddhist writings. Huijiao further pointed out that the purpose of Buddhist writings was to make people "use the snare to get the hare, and rely on the finger to know the moon." To him, language is the snare that enables one to catch the hare (truth), or the finger that points at the moon. "When one knows the moon, then one dispenses with the finger; when one gets the hare, then one forgets the snare."[100] Incidentally, the quotation from the *Lao Zi*, the use of the terms "sage" and "Way" (*dao*), and the borrowing of Zhuang Zi's metaphor of the snare all demonstrate the assimilation of Daoist elements by Chinese Buddhism.

This assimilation culminated in the rise of Chan (Zen), which represents the greatest paradox of all, since it claimed to have originated from Kāśyapa's smile of instant understanding and acknowledged Bodhidharma as its first patriarch in China, who was said to have arrived there from Persia or India, probably about A.D. 480 and to have followed the principles of "not establishing words, pointing directly to the human mind, and revealing one's nature to achieve Buddhahood."[101] The Chan school supposedly practiced "mind-to-mind transmission" (*chuan xin*) without using words, but in fact Chan masters used "public cases" (*gong'an*, Japanese *kōan*), riddlelike questions, to help their disciples achieve enlightenment. They also wrote *gāthā* (*jie*), a kind of hymn, following the prosody of classical Chinese verse (*shi*). Although they often told their disciples not to remember their words, their sayings, verses, and "public cases" were recorded and commented on. This paradox, of course, did not escape the notice of some Chan masters. A drastic reaction against the paradox was Dahui's burning of the printing blocks of the *Biyan lu* (which has been translated into English as "The Blue Cliff Record," although the title would be more accurately rendered "The Green Cliff Record") about 1140.[102] However, manuscript copies of the work, compiled by Dahui's master, Yuanwu, survived. The Confucian scholar Zhou Chi, in his preface (1305) to the reprinted edition of this collection wrote:

> Even when our master [Confucius] understood the Way, he wished to say nothing. How much more so with the Buddhists, who engage in the *Dharma* that would transcend the world: how can it be sought in writing and words? Nevertheless, there are some [writings and words] that cannot be abolished. Wise ones are few, but foolish ones are many; those who have studied are few but those who have not are many. The *Tripiṭaka* contains over five thousand scrolls, all of which are for the benefit of future generations. If one could really forget words, then Śākyamuni and Lao Zi should have kept their mouths shut. Why should they have kept babbling on like this?[103]

This position both shows an acceptance of the paradox of language and provides a rationalization for the publication of the writings of the Chan masters.

It was perhaps no coincidence that Chan flourished during the Tang (618–907) and Song (960–1279) periods, when Chinese poetry enjoyed unprecedented and unsurpassed florescence too. Many poets and critics discussed poetry in Chan terms, as we shall see in chapter 3. However, strictly speaking, "Chan poetics," like "Trappist rhetoric," is a contradiction in terms, since Chan is based on the principle of not relying on words for enlightenment. Although we may speak of "poetry with a Chan flavor" or "poetry influenced by Chan," we should realize that the Chan masters and the poets had different aims: the former used words to trigger enlightenment and advised their disciples to discard the words as soon as they had reached enlightenment, but the latter, by definition, could not discard words, whatever their religious and philosophical orientations may have been.

In general, Chinese intellectuals are usually eclectic or syncretic in their thinking, and it is often difficult to separate Buddhist elements in their thought from Daoist and Confucian ones, since Chan is a synthesis of Buddhism and Daoism, and Neo-Confucianism is a synthesis of all three schools of thought. In any case, I see no point in attempting to separate the different strands of thought in a Chinese writer, any more than attempting to separate the Judeo-Christian strands from the Greco-Roman in the thought of a Western poet or thinker. Unless a Chinese writer makes specific references to Confucianism, Buddhism, or Daoism, I shall deal with his ideas for what they are, without attaching labels to them.

Among post-Tang writers who touched on the paradox of language, Liu Yan (1048–1102) shows an attitude of acceptance. In a letter to Zeng Gong (1019–1083), one of the so-called eight masters of archaic prose of the Tang and the Song, Liu wrote:

> If true principles could be understood without words, and the marvelous Dao could move without a trace, then the world would no longer need to rely on words, and words would no longer have anything with which to respond to the world. It is precisely because of forms and appearances that cannot be described, subtle and abstruse [principles] that cannot be exhausted, what resembles the nature of the myriad things within [oneself], what unifies the changes of the myriad things without, what stimulates clear hearing and vision beside one and enables one to reach, suddenly, the encounter between one's nature and life [on the one hand] and the Dao and its power [on the other] that words may not be stopped and literary works are composed.[104]

This passage shows that the Confucian pragmatic view of literature is not incompatible with the poetics of paradox, for though Liu Yan sees literature primarily as a means of propagating the Dao, he also sees it as an attempt to describe the indescribable.[105]

One of the few Chinese writers who may be suspected of phonocentrism is Yuan Zongdao (1568–1610), who wrote in his essay "Discourse on Literature": "The mouth and the tongue are what represent the heart/mind, and literature is what in turn represents the mouth and the tongue. Being twice removed, even if it is fluently written, it will not, one fears, be as good as the mouth and the tongue. How can it be like what lies in the heart/mind?" However, he then went on to reaffirm the power of writing as a means of communication. "Therefore, Confucius, in discussing literature, said: 'Words communicate; that is all.' The difference between what is literature and what is not lies in whether it communicates or not.[106] The seeming inconsistency is due to the fact that Yuan was fighting against the archaists of his time, who advocated imitation of ancient writers.[107] His aim was to urge that one should write as one would speak, not to downgrade writing as a means of communication.

In the pages above I have presented materials and arguments concerning the paradox of language, in preparation for an examination of the poetics of paradox as it emerged and developed in China. However, before we undertake this task we should first consider the nature of poetics as a metaparadox, the subject of the next chapter.

# The Metaparadox
# of Poetics

Poetry, which represents a particularly heightened and self-conscious use of language, illustrates the paradox of language in a particularly acute form, and poets, being particularly sensitive to language, are often keenly aware of this paradox, especially when they write about the writing of poetry. The same is true of literary theorists and critics who attempt to elucidate the nature of poetry or prescribe rules on how to write poetry; and in traditional China all literary theorists and critics were also poets, even if not very good ones at times. Thus, if poetry is a paradox, then poetics is a metaparadox, and my writing about poetics is a metametaparadox. Someone who then tried to deconstruct my writing would be engaging in a metametametaparadox. It is not my intention to start such an infinite regress—but it is not within my power to prevent it either!

The best example of the metaparadox of poetics in Chinese is the "*Fu* on Literature" (*Wenfu*) by Lu Ji (261–303), especially the preface.[1] Since this preface is crucial to our present concern, I shall try to translate it anew and analyze it in some detail, much translated and annotated though the whole work has been.

Whenever I read the creations of talented authors, I presume to think that I have obtained some insight into the way their minds worked. Now, in issuing words and dispatching phrases, there are indeed numerous variations, yet as to whether it is beautiful or ugly, good or bad, this is something that one can speak of. Whenever I compose a literary work myself, I perceive the nature [of writing] even more keenly, constantly worried that my ideas may not match things or that my words may not capture my ideas, for the difficulty lies not in knowing how, but in being able to do it.

Therefore I have created this '*Fu* on Literature' to describe the luxuriant beauties of former authors, taking this opportunity to discuss the causes of gains or losses in writing. Someday it may perhaps be said to have subtly exhausted the wonders of literature. Although, with regard to holding a wooden-handled axe to cut another axe handle, the model is not far, when it comes to the changes that follow the movement of the hand [in consonance with the working of the mind], these are indeed difficult to capture in words. In general, what can be said in words is all presented here.[2]

In the opening sentence, Lu Ji adopts the reader's point of view and expresses his confidence in his ability to understand not only what former authors wrote but also how their minds worked when they wrote. Next, he affirms the possibility of critical discrimination, in spite of the infinite variety of literature. Both his self-confidence in understanding former authors and his affirmation of the possibility of criticism are based on his own experience as a writer, which enables him to identify with former writers, and this identification in turn enables Lu Ji the poet to write as Lu Ji the critic, without ceasing to be the poet at the same time. After all, the *Wenfu* is as much a tour de force of fine writing as a treatise on the art of writing. He points out that writing is not simply a matter of matching words with things but involves first conceiving or perceiving things and then expressing in words one's own conceptions or perceptions of them. In this matter he shows greater insight than his contempory Ouyang Jian, whose failure to recognize the tripartite relationship among words, ideas, and things we examined in the last chapter. Lu

Ji further points out the difference between knowing in theory how to do a thing and being actually able to do it. If we may illustrate his point with a modern analogy: it is one thing to know in theory what one should do to drive a car, but quite another to be able actually to drive one.

When one tries to write an *ars poetica*, as Lu Ji does here, then to the difficulty of writing is added the difficulty of writing about the difficulty of writing. To continue our homely analogy: it is one thing to be able to drive a car, but quite another to teach someone else to drive. Anyone who writes poetry attempts the seemingly impossible task of describing the indescribable nature of reality, and anyone who writes an *ars poetica* attempts the even more difficult task of describing the indescribable nature of writing. Yet Lu Ji makes precisely such an attempt.

One sentence in the second paragraph quoted above presents a problem: *tuori dai ke wei qu jin qi miao,* translated above as: "Someday it may perhaps be said to have subtly exhausted the wonders of literature." Commentators since Li Shan (ca. 630–689) have taken *tuori* to mean "someday in the future." Qian Zhongshu, however, takes it as a reference to the past and the whole sentence as a reference to the works of former writers.[3] Qian argues that, if we understand this sentence as translated here, it will contradict the statement "these are indeed difficult to capture in words," as well as the line "this is what the wheelwright Pian could not put into words" in the main text that follows. Although, as Qian has demonstrated, *tuori* could refer to the past rather than the future, the sentence in question seems to be placed too far from the mention of "former writers" to refer to them. Moreover, the conjectural term *dai ke* ("may perhaps") seems inappropriate for a reference to the past. If Lu Ji indeed meant to say "in former days these were said to have subtly exhausted the wonders of literature," then why did he use the expression "may perhaps be said"? In any case, if we take "someday" as a reference to the future, the sentence does not necessarily contradict "these are indeed difficult to capture in words" or "this is what the wheelwright Pian could not put into words," for Lu Ji is playing on the paradoxical nature of poetics, first disclaiming the possibility of describing the secrets of the art of writing and then proceeding to make such a description. The sentence "someday it may perhaps be said to have subtly exhausted the wonders of literature" is consistent with the last sentence of the preface: "In general, what can be said in words is all presented here."

The expression "holding a wooden-handled axe to cut another axe handle" is an allusion to a poem in the *Shi jing* (Book, or classic, of poetry), the earliest anthology of Chinese poetry (ca. 1100–ca. 600 B.C.).

> To cut an axe-handle: how?
> No axe, no success.
> To take a wife: how?
> No matchmaker, no getting.
>
> To cut an axe-handle, yea,
> The model is not far.
> I meet this young person;
> The ceremonial vessels are arrayed.[4]

Whereas in the original poem the axe handle represents simply any instrument or means to an end, Lu Ji has turned it into a sophisticated symbol of the metaparadox of poetics: in using poetic language to describe the art of poetry, he is like someone using a wooden-handled axe to cut down a branch and make another wooden axe handle. We shall later see how a contemporary American poet made use of the same symbol.

Lu Ji's allusion to Zhuang Zi's parable of the wheelwright, which we have seen in chapter 1, further illustrates his awareness of the paradoxical nature of language, poetry, and poetics, for the parable is told in words. In short, Lu Ji acknowledges the metaparadox of poetics in the preface and then gives a brilliant demonstration of it in the main text itself. To illustrate this insight, I shall quote from a passage in which Lu Ji describes poetic inspiration and then confesses that he does not understand it.

As for the encounter with inspiration,
The law governing its flow or obstruction—
When it comes, it cannot be checked;
When it goes, it cannot be stopped.
Sometimes it hides itself like light vanishing;
Sometimes it stirs like sound arising.
When the natural trigger is fast and sharp,
What confusion will not be put in order?
Gusts of thought issue forth from the breast,
Fountains of words flow from the lips and teeth:
Luxuriant profusion and powerful splendor
Are captured by the writing brush and white silk.
Words, brilliantly shining, inundate the eye;
Music, richly sounding, fills the ear.
But when the six emotions run sluggish,
When the will strives forward but the spirit delays,
Then [the mind] is unfeeling like a withered tree
And empty like a dried-up stream;
Though one may concentrate one's soul to search the mysteries,
And lift up one's spirit to seek by oneself,
Order, lying in the dark, becomes even more submerged;
Thoughts, obstinately recalcitrant, refuse to be drawn out.
Therefore, sometimes one may exhaust one's feelings but achieve
    regrettable results;
At other times one may follow one's ideas freely yet commit few
    faults.
Even though this matter rests with myself,
It is not within my power to control it.
Thus, often I stroke my empty bosom and sigh,
For I have not understood the causes of its ebb and flow.[5]

A more eloquent example of the metaparadox of poetry is hard to imagine [for here Lu Ji's own eloquence seems powerfully inspired, yet it is eloquence used to articulate what seemingly cannot be articulated].

Among later Chinese poets who perceived the paradoxical nature of poetry was the great Tao Qian (Tao Yuanming, 365–427), as shown by the concluding couplet of what is probably his most famous poem, one in a series of poems entitled "Drinking Wine" (*Yin jiu*; which, however, are not drinking songs but poems written at random after drinking).[6]

> In this there is true meaning;
> I wished to wax eloquent, but have forgotten words.[7]

Although the referent of "this" is not clear, it probably refers to the otherworldly state of mind and the natural environment described in the preceding lines rather than to drinking, for in spite of the collective title, this poem makes no mention of wine. The word translated "wax eloquent" is *bian*, which, as we have seen, can mean both "to speak eloquently, dispute" and "to make distinctions." The dilemma faced by Tao Qian, who has expressed reality as an undifferentiated whole, is the same as that faced by Zhuang Zi: for Tao to convey, in poetry, his sense of the undifferentiated state of reality, he has no resort other than words, which involve the making of distinctions. He resolves the dilemma by accepting Zhuang Zi's advice to "forget words" after getting the "meaning" as well as the latter's paradox, "Great eloquence does not speak."[8] The point of the last line is not so much that the poet wishes to speak but cannot find the words as that he has reached the stage of understanding that no longer requires words. The paradox is, of course, that he has to use words to tell us that he has forgotten words, and since he is writing about his own act of writing this poem, his words may also be taken as an example of the metaparadox of poetics, if we may include in the term "poetics" any writing on poetry, especially poetry on poetry.

Next, I should like to return to Liu Xie. Although he is generally positive about the powers of language and of literature and optimistic about the possibilities of interpretation, he is by no means unaware of the difficulties of writing and of writing about writing. In the chapter called *Shensi*, which I translate as "Intuitive Thought" rather than the more usual "Imagination"(for reasons given elsewhere),[9] Liu Xie writes:

> At the moment when one grasps the writing brush, one's vital spirit is doubly strong before phrases are formed; by the time the piece is completed, half of what one's mind originally conceived has been frustrated. Why so? Ideas turn in the void and can easily be extraordinary, but words bear witness to reality and can achieve artistry only with difficulty. Hence, ideas derive from [intuitive] thought, and words derive from ideas. If they correspond closely, there will be no discrepancy; if they are apart, one will miss by a thousand *li*.[10]

This passage echoes Lu Ji's concern that one's ideas may not match things or one's words may not capture one's ideas, but Liu Xie introduces a further distinction between "idea" (*yi*) and "[intuitive] thought" (*si*). Admittedly, there is no unanimous agreement as to what these terms mean. Wang Yuanhua, for instance, asserts that Liu Xie's three terms *si* ("thought"), *yi* ("idea"), and *yan* ("word") are not the same as the three terms *yi* ("idea"), *xiang* ("image"), and *yan* ("word") used by Wang Bi (226–249), who wrote one of the most important commentaries on the *Book of Changes*.[11] In contrast, Zhou Zhenfu interprets Liu Xie's *yi* as *yixiang* ("mental image").[12] On the whole I am inclined to agree with Wang, since Liu Xie usually uses the word *yi* to mean "idea," and when he does mean "mental image" he uses the binome *yixiang* (granted, only once). On the other hand, I agree with Zhou that the word *si* here is not "ordinary thought" but refers to *shen si*, or "intuitive thought," as indicated in the chapter heading. In the text Liu Xie is abbreviating the term because of the demands of his medium, namely, parallel prose (*pianwen*). Liu Xie's ideas about the interrelationships among reality, perception, language, and literature are quite complicated; I have attempted to elucidate some of them elsewhere and shall not repeat myself here.[13]

In the same chapter Liu Xie further remarks:

> As for subtle intentions beyond thought and oblique moods beyond writing, these are what words cannot pursue and what the brush knows it should stop to write about. To reach the ultimate of subtleties and then expound their wonders, to reach the ultimate of changes and then communicate their workings: even Yi Zhi could not speak of the cooking cauldron, nor could the wheelwright Pian talk about the axe. Is it not abstruse indeed?[14]

Liu Xie's awareness of the metaparadox of poetics is also preceptible in the postface (*Xuzhi*, or "Relating My Intention"), which comes at the end of the book, although it is placed at the beginning [as if it were an introduction—a purpose it well serves] by Vincent Shih in his translation. After congratulating himself on the comprehensiveness of his work, Liu Xie adds with uncharacteristic modesty: "However, 'words do not exhaust meaning': even the sage [Confucius] found difficulties therein. My knowledge being limited to the capacity of a pitcher or the view from a pipe,[15] how can I lay down laws with squares and rulers? Now that the remote ages of the past have purified my hearing, perhaps the distant generations of the future may pollute their sight with my work."[16] From the author of the greatest *ars poetica* ever written in Chinese, this must be considered a handsome admission of the metaparadox of poetics.

In the works of later writers, we see from time to time indications that they are aware of the paradoxical nature of poetry, if not poetics. The Neo-Confucian philosopher Shao Yong (courtesy name Yaofu, 1001–1077), who held generally pragmatic views on literature,[17] nonetheless wrote in one of his "Head and Tail Songs" (*Shou wei yin*):

Not that I, Yaofu, love to compose poetry;
When poetry reaches "forgetting words," then it is time to stop.
Although we borrow words to communicate the essential and
    marvelous,
We also need to see the subtle and abstruse from things.

It's only because the broth is unseasoned that we know its bland taste;

Only when the music becomes soundless do we recognize its inaudible qualities.

How many scenes of breezes and flowers await deletion and revision!

Not that I, Yaofu, love to compose poetry.[18]

The first line, which recalls Mencius's remark, "How can I be fond of disputing? I just cannot help it,"[19] together with the next line, presents the paradox that Shao cannot help writing poetry, although he would like to "forget words," as Zhuang Zi advised. In the next couplet, he suggests that language is necessary but not sufficient: we need language to communicate the essential and marvelous nature of things, but we also need to observe things themselves in order to perceive the subtle and abstruse principles underlying them. The next couplet echoes various earlier writers: Lu Ji, who in his "*Fu* on Literature" deplored writings that "lacked the lingering taste of the 'supreme broth' [which was unseasoned]";[20] Tao Qian, who reputedly played on a zither without strings;[21] and Sikong Tu (837–908), who advocated "flavor beyond saltiness and sourness."[22] How Sikong and his followers in later ages developed an aesthetics of paradox will be discussed in the next chapter. Returning now to Shao Yong's poem, we note that the phrase "deletion and revision" (*chugai*), which smacks of a schoolmaster's correction of pupils' essays, seems to suggest that nature [the object of such activity] is a prototext that needs human art to turn it into poetic text. In other words, poetry is not an imitation of nature but an improvement on it.

In view of the above, we may question a statement made by D. W. Fokkema in his article "Chinese and Renaissance Artes Poeticae."

In the Chinese tradition poetry did not claim the right to embellish nature as did "la doctrine classique," nor would a Chinese critic say that "art charms us more than nature does" ("l'Art nous

ravit plus que ne fait la nature") as Demartes maintained in 1640.
. . . The competitive opposition between man and the supernatural in Western civilization has produced consequences in Renaissance poetics, which one will not easily find in Chinese poetics.
The specific problem of imitation (should poetry imitate nature,
or should it idealize it?) may have been produced by the competitive relationship between artist and universe.[23]

While I completely agree with Fokkema that, in traditional
Chinese thinking, human beings are not conceived of as
competing with nature or the supernatural, I must point out
at the same time that some Chinese poets and critics did express the view that poetry could complement or supplement
nature's work. Before Shao Yong, the poet Li He (790–816)
had praised two elder poets by saying, "Their writing
brushes supplement creation: Heaven has no merit."[24] This
famous line has been compared by Qian Zhongshu with various Western parallels, which need not be repeated here.[25]
We may add that many Chinese poets and artists have been
praised with the expression *qiao duo tian gong*, which may be
rendered "his skill forcibly surpasses Heaven's craftsman-
ship," for though the word *duo* literally means "take by
force" or "snatch away," it can also mean "forcibly surpass"
or "usurp," as in Confucius's remark "We dislike purple's
forcibly surpassing [or usurping] red."[26] In any event, the
question remains whether the idea that art can improve on
nature is necessarily rooted in the concept that one's relationship with nature is competitive.

A remarkable example of the metaparadox of poetics is
provided by Jiang Kui (ca. 1155–1221)—poet, composer,
critic, calligrapher, and connoisseur of all the finer things of
life—in the concluding passage of his brief but interesting
treatise *Baishi Daoren shishuo* (The white-stone Daoist's discourse on poetry):

This "Discourse on Poetry" is written not for those who are able
to write poetry but for those who are not able to write poetry, so
as to make them able to write poetry. If they become able to write

poetry and later fully put into effect my "Discourse," then it may be said to be for those who are able to write poetry as well. However, if someone takes my "Discourse" as exhaustive and does not reach his own understanding, how can that be sufficient for "being able to write poetry"? Among enlightened ones in posterity, would there be those who "throw water into water"? Would there be those who would "forget the snare after getting the rabbit"? Alas, my "Discourse" has already offended the poets of the past. May posterity not be offended by me again![27]

By playing on the polysemy of the word *jin*, which, as we have seen, can mean "fully express," or "depleted," or "finish," Jiang Kui indicates that, if one can fully put into effect (*jin*) his discourse on poetry, one will be able to write poetry, but if one thinks that this discourse has exhausted (*jin*) all the secrets of poetry, one will not be a true poet. The discourse points at the way of poetry but is not itself the goal. Jiang expresses himself by means of two allusions. First, he alludes to the passage from the *Lie Zi* quoted in the preceding chapter, where the fictional Confucius told the duke of Bai that a discerning listener could detect a speaker's true intent from subtle hints, just as the famous cook Yiya could tell the difference in taste between the water from one river and that of another. By applying this analogy to poetry and poetics, Jiang Kui suggests that a discerning reader of poetry can detect the poet's true intent from subtle hints, and furthermore, that a discerning reader of the discourse can detect the secrets of poetry from Jiang's subtle hints.

Jiang then alludes to Zhuang Zi's parable about forgetting the trap after getting the fish or forgetting the snare after getting the rabbit. Apart from a slight confusion between "trap" (*quan*, which some commentators take to mean "bait" instead of "trap") and "snare" (*ti*), Jiang makes it quite clear that he wishes his readers to discard his words as soon as they have reached poetic enlightenment, just as Chan masters told their disciples to forget their words as one would discard a raft after reaching the shore, and as, centuries later and in a different world, Ludwig Wittgenstein was to advise his readers to discard his words as one would a ladder after having climbed up it.[28]

Not everyone understood the fish trap, the rabbit snare, and the raft in quite the same way. For instance, He Jingming (1483–1521), who was by and large an archaist but who deplored what he saw as slavish imitation of the ancients in the works of his fellow poet Li Mengyang (1472–1529), wrote to the latter, advising him to discard his models as one would a raft after reaching the shore."Buddha had the analogy of the raft, meaning that when you discard the raft, then you have reached the shore, and when you have reached the shore, then you discard the raft."[29] He Jingming is not using the raft as a metaphor for all language, but only as one for the poetry of the ancients, which he thinks one should discard after reaching poetic enlightenment. But even this modest proposal was rejected by Li Mengyang, who replied: "Now, the raft and I are two, just as the rabbit and the snare or the fish and the trap: one may indeed discard it [the raft]. But the compasses and the carpenter's square are what the circle and the square originate from: even if one wishes to discard them, how can one?"[30]

To He Jingming, the poetry of the ancients, especially that of the great Du Fu (712–770), embodied the natural laws of poetry, and one could no more write poetry without following these laws than one could draw a circle without using compasses or a square without using a carpenter's square. Only the supreme poet, Du Fu, could dispense with the compasses and the carpenter's square, as Li was reported to have said. "In writing poetry one must imitate Du Fu. When poetry reaches Du Fu's stage, it is like a perfect circle to which one can no longer apply the compasses, or a perfect square to which one can no longer apply the carpenter's square."[31] In a letter to someone else, Li expresses similar ideas:

Writing [wen] must have laws and models before it can fit and harmonize with musical measures, as circles and squares in relation to the compasses and the carpenter's square. The ancients used them [laws and models], not because they themselves made them, but because these were really created by Heaven. When people today follow the ancients as laws and models, they are not following the ancients, but really following the natural rules of things.[32]

This position is remarkably similar to Alexander Pope's assertion in "An Essay on Criticism."

> Those Rules of old discovered, not devised,
> Are nature still, but natured methodized.[33]

And Li's claim that Du Fu's poetry embodied natural laws is similar to Pope's claim that Virgil found that Homer and nature were the same:

> When first young Maro in his boundless mind
> A work t'outlast immortal Rome designed,
> Perhaps he seemed above the critic's law,
> And but from nature's fountains scorned to draw:
> But when t'examine every part he came,
> Nature and Homer were, he found, the same.[34]

Both the Chinese archaist and the English neoclassicist have unwittingly presented us with another paradox about poetry: perfect art is identical with nature and therefore, in a sense, no art at all.

The metaphor of the raft was given a twist by the poet-critic Qian Qianyi (1582–1664), who gave up writing poetry after embracing Buddhism but, as we shall have occasion to see later, did not quite give up writing about poetry. In a letter to Fang Wen (Fang Erzhi, 1612–1669), Qian wrote: "The metaphor of the raft in the *Diamond* [*Sūtra*] lays special emphasis on discarding and renouncing. . . . If you, late in life, can renounce poetry and enter the Way [i.e. the Noble Path of Buddhism], you may use this word of mine as a metaphorical raft."[35] It is ironic that a poet should advise another poet to renounce poetry, yet the advice is given in a letter couched in elegant language, with many references to classical Chinese poetry.

In contrast to Qian Qianyi, Wang Shizhen (Wang Yuyang, 1634–1711, not to be confused with another poet-critic, Wang Shizhen, or Wang Yuanmei, 1529–1590) [agreed with He Jingming and] reaffirmed the validity of the raft as an analogy for poetics. " 'To discard the raft and climb ashore' is what experts in Chan consider to be the 'awakened [enlightened] state' [*wujing*] and what experts in poetry considered to be the 'transformed state' [*huajing*]. Poetry and Chan are the same and there is no difference between them. [Tafu (He Jingming) brought this up in a letter he wrote to Kongtong (Li Mengyang).]"[36] It is not clear whether Wang Shizhen meant that the *process* of enlightenment or that the resultant *mental state* of the one was identical with that of the other.[37] In either case, the statement implicitly accepts the metaparadox of poetics as the necessary, albeit ultimately expendable, means to poetic enlightenment.

We may now turn to examples of Western poets who evinced an awareness of the paradox of poetry. Dante's remark that language is conquered by thought ("Il parlare per lo pensiero è vinto")[38] reminds one of Lu Ji's constant worry that one's words might not capture one's ideas. Edmund Spenser illustrates the paradox of poetry when he first claims that he cannot find a fitting comparison for the sun and then proceeds to produce one.

> That may well seemen true; for well I weene,
> That this same day when she on Arlo sat,
> Her garment was so bright and wondrous sheene,
> That my fraile wit cannot devize to what
> It to compare, nor finde like stuffe to that:
> As those three sacred Saints, though else most wise,
> Yet on Mount Thabor quite their wits forgot,
> When they their glorious Lord in strange disguise
> Transfigur'd sawe, his garments so did daze their eyes.[39]

A more striking example occurs in Christopher Marlowe's *Tamburlaine*.

> If all the pens that ever poets held
> Had fed the feeling of their masters' thoughts,
> And every sweetness that inspir'd their hearts,
> Their minds and muses on admired themes;
> If all the heavenly quintessence they still
> From their immortal flowers of poesy,
> Wherein as in a mirror we perceive
> The highest reaches of a human wit—
> If all these had made one poem's period,
> And all combin'd in beauty's worthiness,
> Yet should these hover in their restless heads
> One thought, one grace, one wonder, at the least
> Which into words no virtue can digest.[40]

This apparent complaint that language cannot adequately express a poet's sense of beauty has been hailed by another poet, A. C. Swinburne, as "one of the noblest passages, perhaps indeed the noblest in the literature of the world, ever written by one of the greatest masters of poetry in loving praise of the glorious delights and sublime submission to the everlasting limits of his art"[41]—a tribute couched in paradoxical language that clearly reveals both poets' consciousness of the paradox of poetry.

Shakespeare also seemed aware of this same paradox when in one sonnet he assured his friend,

> So long as men can breathe or eyes can see
> So long lives this, and this gives life to thee.[42]

In another sonnet he feigns inability to describe beauty.

> For we, which now behold these present days,
> Have eyes to wonder, but lack tongues to praise.[43]

When these passages from Marlowe and Shakespeare were cited to illustrate the paradox of poetry at a meeting of com-

parativist literature specialists a few years ago,[44] it prompted
A. Owen Aldridge to make the following comment:

> Liu associated his paradox with the "proud conceit" of the Ren-
> aissance, that is, the statement that a person or a concept will live
> forever because it is enshrined in a poet's verses but, in my opin-
> ion, this favorite conceit of Petrach and Shakespeare actually as-
> serts the enduring power of language. A long passage from Mar-
> lowe's *Tamburlaine* which Liu quoted as a statement of the
> inadequacy of language could be interpreted instead as a tribute
> to the power of the human mind, which keeps on working after
> the words in an artistic creation have already been set down.[45]

In reply, two things can be said. First, the *juxtaposition* of the
"proud conceit" and the professed inability to express oneself constitutes the paradox of poetry; the former alone, of
course, would merely affirm the power of language. Second,
precisely the same point makes the passage from Marlowe an
illustration of the paradox of poetry: had Marlowe only asserted the power of the human mind (which is a major concern of both parts of *Tamburlaine* as well as *Doctor Faustus*),
without at the same time complaining that language was inadequate to express what he wanted to say, there would, of
course, have been no paradox at all. The fact that Swinburne
seized on this passage with such enthusiasm indicates that
he clearly saw and agreed with the paradoxical point it was
making.

Among modern Western poets, Stéphene Mallarmé and
T. S. Eliot are conspicuous for their consciousness of the paradox of poetry. Mallarmé believed in the incantatory power
of poetic language, which he thought could create a new reality, yet sometimes he despaired over the apparent impotence
of language as he sat facing a blank sheet of paper, crying,
"Rien!" ("Nothing!")[46] In the end he seems to have accepted
the paradox as inevitable, for he remarked to his friend Camille Mauclair: "But we are all failures, Mauclair! How can
we be otherwise, when we measure our finiteness against in-

finity?"[47] This admission of "failure," which reminds one of Zhuang Zi's remark "Our lives are finite, but knowledge is infinite; to pursue the infinite with the finite is exhausting,"[48] is in fact an acceptance of the challenge of poetry as an attempt to express the inexpressible.

Eliot's awareness of the paradox of poetry permeates his *Four Quartets*, as can be seen from these well-known lines:

> Words move, music moves
> Only in time; but that which is only living
> Can only die. Words, after speech, reach
> Into the silence. Only by the form, the pattern,
> Can words or music reach
> The stillness, as a Chinese jar still
> Moves perpetually in its stillness.[49]

Also, as Zhuang Zi remarked, "words have never had constancy," so did Eliot complain about the instability of words:

> Words strain,
> Crack and sometimes break, under the burden,
> Under the tension, slip, slide, perish,
> Decay with imprecision, will not stay in place,
> Will not stay still.[50]

Furthermore, Eliot confessed that:

> every attempt
> Is a wholly new start, and a different kind of failure.[51]

This admission is similar to Mallarmé's confession, except that Eliot's is even more remarkable, since his confession of failure is made in admirable verse.

If we use the word "poetry" in a wider sense (like *Dichtung*) to include drama, then some twentieth-century dramatists provide further illustrations of the paradox of poetry. Jean-Paul Sartre's *Huis clos* and Eugene Ionesco's *The Bald Soprano* are both about the inability of human beings to communicate with each other in language, yet the fact that they

wrote these plays suggests a belief in the possibility of communication with the audience. Samuel Beckett is an even better illustration. When he was asked about the contradiction
between his writing and his obvious conviction that language
could not convey meaning, he replied: "Que voulez-vous,
Monsieur? C'est les mots; on n'a rien d'autre."[52] According
to Martin Esslin, "Beckett's whole work is an endeavor to
name the unnameable," and "he may have devaluated language as an instrument for the communication of ultimate
truths, but he has shown himself a great master of language
as an artistic medium."[53] Or, as Floyd Merrell remarked,
"Beckett's characters always fail in their search for an expression of the ineffable because they cannot overcome the im-
mediate limitations of language. And they inexorably continue to talk because, on another plane, language is
potentially limitless."[54] Are we not all in the same boat as
Beckett's characters?

Since at the beginning of this chapter I quoted Lu Ji's use
of the wooden-handled axe as a symbol of the metaparadox
of poetics, it is perhaps appropriate to end the chapter with
a reference to Gary Synder's use of the same symbol. Not
only did Synder name his recent collection of poems "Axe
handles," but he also quoted Lu Ji, while acknowledging his
indebtedness to Ezra Pound and to Ch'en Shih-hsiang, who
translated the *Wenfu* and taught Synder Chinese. However,
there is an interesting difference between Lu Ji and Synder.
Whereras the former saw the wooden axe handle in a paradoxical light, the latter, perhaps with typical American opti-
mism, sees it in a more positive light, as a symbol of the craft
of poetry being transmitted from one generation to the next.
Synder declares that Pound, Ch'en, and himself are all axe
handles, as he now shows his son how to make one.[55]

# 3

## The Poetics
## of Paradox

The awareness of the paradoxical nature of language and of poetry led Chinese poets not to abandon poetry but instead to develop a poetics of paradox, which may be summarized as the principle of saying more by saying less, or, in its extreme form, saying all by saying nothing. In practice, this poetics manifested itself in the preference shown by many poets and critics for implicitness over explicitness, conciseness over verbosity, obliqueness over directness, and suggestion over description.

Before presenting the poetics of paradox, I should like first to tell an anecdote that illustrates how the principle of the poetics of paradox supposedly worked in real life. The anecdote concerns three famous poets: Cao Cao (155–220), who was nominally prime minister of Han but virtually the ruler of the empire; his eldest son, Cao Pi (187–226), who took over the throne from the last Han emperor and founded the Wei dynasty, honored his father posthumously as Emperor Wu of Wei, and was himself known posthumously as Emperor Wen; and Cao Pi's younger brother, Cao Zhi (192–232), who is generally considered the most gifted poet of the three. According to Pei Songzhi (372–451), who wrote the standard commentary on *History of the Three Kingdoms* (*Sanguo zhi*) by Chen Shou (233–297), which includes the official *History of the Wei* (*Wei shu*), once, when Cao Cao, as prince of Wei, was leaving the capital on a military campaign, his heir apparent,

Cao Pi, and younger brother, Cao Zhi, both saw him off. Cao Zhi spoke eloquently in praise of his father, and the prince was pleased. Cao Pi felt at a loss, whereupon one of his advisors, Wu Zhi, whispered to him, "The prince is due to leave; you may shed tears." So the heir apparent wept and bowed without saying anything, and the prince thought he was more sincere than his younger brother.[1]

One interesting feature of the poetics of paradox in the Chinese tradition is that those who advocated it were fond of drawing analogies between poetry and music and poetry and food. The analogy between poetry and music should come as no surprise to any Western reader, although it may be worthwhile pointing out that, in China, music and poetry were more closely related to each other than in the West and that most Chinese poetic genres originated as songs identified with a particular type of music.

The analogy between poetry and food may seem strange to some Western readers, for though in Western languages one may speak of "taste" or "gout" or "gustibus," it is not so common to find critics actually comparing poetry to food. Even when one speaks of "food for thought," one is thinking of spiritual sustenance rather than flavor. In contrast, the great importance attached to cuisine in Chinese culture makes the comparison of poetry to food seem perfectly natural, if not inevitable. [In fact, many activities in traditional China were often compared analogously with cooking and food. For instance,] the word *zai*, which may occur by itself, although more commonly as part of a compound such as *zaixiang* or *taizai*, and which is conventionally translated "prime minister" or "chief minister," literally means "to slaughter," and Paul Kroll has gone as far as to translate *zaixiang* as "mectatory minister," namely, one concerned with "mectation," or the ritual slaughtering of animals [a ritual that in earliest times the holder of this office actually performed].[2] Apart from etymology, the task of the chief minister was often compared to that of the master chef: the former had to harmonize diverse elements in society, just as the latter had to harmonize diverse ingredients in the cooking cauldron, and both were supposed to maintain a balance between the forces of *yin* and *yang* [the negative and positive cosmic forces].

Those who drew an analogy between poetry and music while expounding the poetics of paradox must have been aware of certain passages in the *Lao Zi* and the *Zhuang Zi*. In the former (chapter 41) we read that "great music is inaudible,"[3] and in the latter (chapter 2) we encounter the following parable: "There were completions and omissions: that was when Master Zhao of old played the zither. There were no completions nor omissions: that was when Master Zhao of old did not play the zither."[4] This translation is based on Xuan Ying's commentary, which bears a preface dated 1721 and was first published in 1867. Xuan glossed the character *gu* ("therefore") by a homophone *gu* ("ancient," or "of old").[5] Most other commentators interpret the character as "therefore," and an alternative rendering of the passage would be: "There were completions and omissions: that was why Master Zhao played the zither. There were no completions nor omissions: that was why Master Zhao did not play the zither."[6] "Master Zhao" refers to Zhao Wen, mentioned in the next sentence in the text, an expert player of the zither (*qin*). The point of the parable is that, if one plays the zither— no matter how skillfully—one may complete one tune while missing all other potential tunes, whereas if one does not play the zither, no tune will be completed and no tune will be missed.[7] For this reason, as mentioned in the preceding chapter, Tao Qian played on a zither without strings.

The poetics of paradox may be said to have emerged during the Tang period, the golden age of Chinese poetry, although hints at such a poetics are already discernible in Liu Xie's *The Literary Mind*. In the chapter entitled "Concealed and Prominent Beauties" (*Yinxiu*), he writes:

Among literary flowers, there are prominent ones and concealed ones. What is called "concealed" refers to multiple meanings beyond words; what is called "prominent" refers to expressions that stand out in a piece. . . . The nature of concealed beauty lies in the fact that meaning is born beyond words: secret echoes resonate on all sides, and hidden colors issue forth from their submergence. This is comparable to the way the broken and unbroken lines of the hexagrams alternate their forms, or the rivers and streams harbor pearls and jade.[8]

Although Liu Xie does not advocate "concealed beauty" exclusively, he does recognize it as one of the two main kinds of literary beauty. According to him, concealed beauty can evoke resonances beyond words, just as the broken and unbroken lines of the hexagrams in the *Book of Changes* can reveal the underlying mysteries of the universe. This passage foreshadows many later writings that advocate meaning beyond words.

Among Tang poets, one of the first to herald the poetics of paradox was Wang Changling (ca. 690–ca. 756), whose treatise on poetry, "Models of Poetry" (*Shige*), has survived in fragments preserved in the "Discourse on the Secret Treasury of the Mirror of Literature" (*Wenjing mifu lun*, or [in Japanese] *Bunkyō hifuron*), compiled by the Japanese Buddhist monk Kūkai (also known as Kōbō Daishi, 773–834), who had studied in China. In this work we find various quotations from Wang Changling's lost work that evince a preference for conciseness and suggestiveness over verbosity and explicit description. In one passage, Wang claims that the most ancient poetry is the best because "the meaning can be seen in one line," whereas in later poetry it requires two or even four lines to reveal the meaning.[9] In another passage he writes: "In all poetry, what combines description of objects with meaning is good. If there is description of objects but no meaning or inspired mood, then even if it is skillful, there is no place for it."[10] Both the basic idea and the phraseology foreshadow numerous later critics. In yet another passage

Wang writes, "The concluding line must make one feel as if the thought had never ended: only then is it good."[11] This view anticipates later critics such as Jiang Kui and Yan Yu.

In practice, the poetics of paradox is well exemplified by the poetry of Wang Wei (701–761), which, at its best and most typical, is characterized by conciseness, suggestiveness, and implicitness. These qualities are particularly noticeable in some of his famous concluding couplets, such as:

> You ask reasons for adversity or success—
> The fisherman's song enters deeply into the shore.[12]

The last line is a non sequitur, which may be interpreted as a hint that the fisherman's song embodies all the wisdom that the interlocutor might wish for, or as a riddle, a Chan *gong'an* (*kōan*) intended to shock one into enlightenment.[13] In either case, the apparent nonanswer seems more effective than any explicit answer could be.

That Wang Wei was aware of the poetics of paradox can also be seen in his "Preface to *Poems on Flowers and Medicinal Herbs* by the Reverend Master Guang of Jianfu Monastery," in which he deliberately turns the principle of saying more by saying less upside down. "There is nothing in which the Way [Dao] does not reside; so how can things be worth forgetting? Hence, the more he sings and chants of these things, the more I perceive his silence."[14] Behind this statement is Zhuang Zi's paradox that to speak is the same as not to speak. Accepting this paradox provides an excuse for writing poetry, even if one admits the futility of language.

The paradox of answering a question by not answering is also present in the well-known quatrain by Li Bai [or Li Bo] (701–762).

### Question and Answer in the Mountains

> You ask me why I nestle among the green mountains;
> I smile without answering, my mind, by itself, at ease.
> Peach blossoms on flowing water are going far away:
> There is another cosmos, not the human world.[15]

Here again, the last line, a seeming non sequitur, is more effective than any direct answer.

Another well-known poem, by Liu Changqing (709–780), may also illustrate the poetics of paradox.

*Seeking the Daoist Priest Chang Shan's Retreat at South Stream*

> All along the way, where I've passed,
> The moss reveals sandals' traces.
> White clouds cling to quiet isles;
> Fragrant grass shuts the unused gate.
> After rain, I view the pines' color;
> Following the mountain, I reach the water's source.
> Riverside flowers and Chan's meaning—
> Face to face, also forgetting words.[16]

The last two lines are ambiguous. In the penultimate, the word *yu* can be taken as "and," as in the above translation, or as "share," "participate," or "join." In the last line, the subjects of *xiangdui* ("face each other") and *wang yan* ("forget words") are not identified: it is possible to take "riverside flowers" and "Chan's meaning" as the implied subjects, but it makes better sense to assume that the flowers and the speaker are the implied subjects. Another suggestion, that the speaker and the Daoist priest are the subjects, seems implausible, since the priest is absent—indeed, the whole point of the poem is that it is *not* necessary for the speaker to see the object of the search, the journey itself and the surroundings reached being sufficient rewards. (Many other poems on similar subjects make a similar point.) In view of the above, the last two lines may now be rendered:

> Riverside flowers share Chan's meaning:
> Facing each other, we too forget words.

A translation of these lines by Jerome Seaton is too free:

> Flowers in the stream reveal Ch'an's meaning.
> Face to face, and all words gone.[17]

There is no reason to think that the flowers are "in the stream" instead of "by the stream," and nothing in the text warrants reading "reveal" into the text. Furthermore, "forget words" is not quite the same as "all words gone." The speaker has followed Zhuang Zi's advice to "get the meaning and forget the words," yet he has to use words to tell us this. As Francois Cheng pointed out, the ending of this poem is similar to that of one of Tao Qian's "Drinking Wine" poems, which I quoted in the previous chapter.

> In this there is a true meaning;
> I wished to wax eloquent, but have forgotten words.

Cheng's comments form a variation on the poetics of paradox. "Thus the two poems are not 'descriptive' in nature; they are in themselves an experience of wordlessness through words, an 'initiation' into 'pure significance.' "[18]

More explicit evidence of the poetics of paradox can be seen in the prose writings of the Buddhist monk Jiaoran (730–799), such as in the following passage from his "Exempla of Poetry" (*Shishi*): "As for spontaneously outstanding lines, they compete with Creation: they may be groped into by the imagination but are hard to describe in words. Unless one is a true writer, one cannot know this."[19] This awareness of the paradox of poetics did not prevent him from prescribing rules for writing poetry. However, under the heading, "There are two things to be rejected in poetry," he writes: "Although one would wish to reject skill and advocate straightforwardness, the process of thought cannot be put aside. Although one would wish to reject words and advocate meaning, classical beauty cannot be omitted."[20]

It seems that he saw wordless poetry as an ideal, but realized that in practice one could not do without words. Nonetheless, he advocated meaning beyond words, even though he disagreed with Wang Changling that the most ancient poetry should be esteemed the most because the meaning could be seen in one line.[21] In the passage entitled "Examples of poetry with multiple meanings," Jiaoran writes: "All [poetry]

that has twofold meaning or more expresses intention beyond words. If one encounters a superior master like the
duke of Kangle [Xie Lingyun, 385–443] and observes [his po-
etry], one will see only his emotion and nature, but will not
see any words. This is because he has reached the ultimate
of the Way [Dao]."[22] It was no accident that Jiaoran chose Xie
Lingyun as an exemplary master of poetry, for Xie was his
ancestor. (This relationship is not apparent, because Chinese
Buddhist monks renounce their surnames; Jiaoran's name
before he became a monk was Xie Zhou.)

Furthermore, Jiaoran gives examples of manifold meaning
as follows:

#### TWOFOLD MEANING

Song Yu [ca. 290–ca. 223 B.C.]:

> Bright like a beautiful lady,
> Lifting her sleeve to shield the sun and gazing
> toward the one she longs for.

Cao Zijian [Cao Zhi]:

> The lofty tower is full of sad wind;
> The morning sun shines on the northern wood.

Wang Wei:

> The autumn wind is just now desolate;
> Retainers disperse from the prince of Mengchang's gate.

Wang Changling:

> Feelings of parting here beyond the cries of apes,
> Sky cold, the Gui River long.

#### THREEFOLD MEANING

"Ancient Poem" [anonymous, first or second century B.C.]:

> A floating cloud covers the white sun;
> The wanderer does not think of returning home.

FOURFOLD MEANING

"Ancient Poem" [anonymous, first or second century B.C.]:

> On and on, again on and on:
> To you I said lifelong farewell.

Song Yu's "Nine Arguments" [*Jiubian*]:

> Sad and forlorn, Oh, as if traveling far,
> Climbing a mountain and overlooking the water to
>     see off someone going home.[23]

Jiaoran unfortunately gives no explanation for any of this, and the lines quoted are themselves of little help.

Under "Twofold Meaning," the first quotation is from the "*Fu* on the Gaotang Tower" (*Gaotang fu*), attributed to Song Yu, and is part of a description of the goddess of Mount Wu, with whom the king of Chu is supposed to have had an amorous encounter in a dream.[24] Traditional critics have interpreted the work as moral allegory, so perhaps Jiaoran had in mind a literal meaning combined together with an allegorical or tropological meaning. (The term "allegory" as applied to Chinese poetry raises certain problems, but we cannot go into them here.)[25]

The second quotation is from one of the "Miscellaneous Poems" (*Zashi*) by Cao Zhi and has been interpreted by the commentator Li Shan as follows: "The lofty tower is an analogy for the capital; the sad wind refers to edicts; the morning sun is an analogy for the emperor's bright understanding; the northern wood refers to narrowness, and is an analogy for petty men."[26] Far-fetched as this interpretation may seem to us, Jiaoran may well have accepted it as a second level of meaning.

The third and fourth quotations are both a farewell. The former is from Wang Wei's "Sending Off Administrator Yuan of Qizhou, Who Is Returning Home" (*Song Qizhou Yuan zhangshi gui*)[27] and contains an allusion to the prince of Mengchang, a feudal lord of the third century B.C. who was famous for his patronage of able men. Wang Wei's own head-note states that he and Yuan were formerly both on the staff of the late "Senior Palace Attendant Cui," and the point of the allusion seems to be no more than that both the poet and his friend have lost a generous patron. The latter quotation is from Wang Changling's "Sending Off Tan the Eighth, Who Is Going to Guilin" (*Song Tan Ba zhi Guilin*), a perfectly conventional farewell poem.[28] It is difficult to know what kind of twofold meaning Jiaoran saw in these two couplets.

The single example given of threefold meaning is from a group of poems known collectively as the "Nineteen Ancient Poems," which first seem to have appeared together in the *Literary Anthology* (*Wenxuan*) compiled by Xiao Tong, posthumously entitled Crown Prince Zhaoming (501–531).[29] The poem in question can be interpreted on three levels.[30] On the literal level, the poem expresses the feelings of a woman whose husband is wandering far away and has not come home, and the line "a floating cloud covers the white sun" can be taken as a description of a natural phenomenon. On another level, the cloud can be taken as representing a rival, who hides the erring husband, represented by the sun; alternatively, the cloud may represent something that momentarily "clouds" the husband's reason, while the sun may represent his normal, rational mind. (These are my own conjectures.) On a third level, as some traditional critics have suggested, the cloud may represent the ubiquitous "petty men," while the sun may represent the ruler.[31]

The first example under "Fourfold Meaning" is the opening couplet of this same anonymous poem. I fail to see what fourfold meaning it could possibly contain. The second example is from a melancholy poem that may have allegorical significance, but again I cannot find four distinct levels of meaning in it.[32]

In brief, although we cannot be sure what Jiaoran meant by "twofold meaning," "threefold meaning," and "fourfold meaning," he evidently seems to have seen a link between the ideal of wordless poetry and the practice of using words in such a way as to suggest multiple levels of meaning and meaning beyond words. He may therefore be said to have anticipated not only later Chinese critics but also some Western ones who emphasized "ambiguity" or "plurisignation."

The poetics of paradox found its most radical as well as most elegant expression in Sikong Tu's *Twenty-Four Moods of Poetry* (*Ershisi shipin*), a sequence of twenty-four poems in archaic tetrasyllabic verse, which has been interpreted in widely divergent ways. For my own part, I cannot accept Bruno Belpaire's interpretation of this sequence of poems as a Daoist regimen for spiritual self-cultivation,[33] for the poems, after all, are explicitly concerned with poetry; nor do I find it necessary, as did Du Songbo, to interpret these poems in exclusively Chan Buddhist terms.[34] In any case, here we cannot discuss the sequence as a whole but only focus our attention on the famous dictum epitomizing the poetics of paradox that occurs in the poem entitled *Hanxu*, which has been translated "Conservation" by H. A. Giles, "Contenir une masse (d'éléments étrangers)" by Bruno Belpaire, "The Pregnant Mode" by Yang Hsien-yi and Gladys Yang, "Reserve" by Wai-lim Yip, and "Potentiality" by Pauline Yu.[35] I think "Reserve" is the best translation, since it means both "holding back" (*han*) and "storing up" (*xu*)—by being "reserved" in words, one can build up a "reserve" of meaning.

The dictum itself bristles with difficulties of interpretation and translation: *bu zhuo* [or *zhu*] *yi zi / jin de fengliu*. The first character is a negative particle, corresponding to "not" or "without"; the second character, which can be pronounced *zhuo* or *zhu*, can mean "put down," "adhere to," or "write"; the third and fourth characters together mean "one word" or "one written character." Thus, the first half of the dictum is generally understood to mean, "not putting down a single word" or "without putting down a single word," although Xiao Shuishun interpreted it as "not a word in the poem is stuck [*nienzhuo*]," and Richard John Lynn rendered it as "not becoming attached to a single word."[36] We shall consider this point below.

In the second half of the dictum, *jin* and *de* together mean "fully obtain" and present no problem; *fengliu*, literally "wind-flow," which may be taken as "the wind's flow" or "the wind and the flow of water," has a range of meanings, from "free-spirited and unconventional" to "romantically amorous." As used by Sikong Tu, I do not think the term means "wit" (Giles), "beauty" (Yang and Yang), "flowing grace" (Yip, who adds a note that it refers to "Taoist-tinctured way of living"), "elegant style" (Yu), or "charisma" (Zhang Longxi), but means something like the "dynamic force" or "life-rhythm" of nature.[37] My interpretation is supported by such dictionaries as the *Cihai* (Ocean of phrases), which cites the lines in question and defines the term *fengliu* as "the quintessential spirit, the tone or flavor, which cannot be sought from traces or appearances."[38]

We may now consider both halves of the dictum together. Obviously, we cannot take the lines literally and simply to mean "without writing down a single word, one can capture the dynamic force of nature." However, Qian Zhongshu interprets the first part this way: " 'Not putting down' means 'not putting down more' or 'not putting down again.' Having put down some words, one can then [practice] 'not putting down a single word,' to use silence to assist words, making the mutually contradictory mutually complementary: how can this be the same as 'non-speaking, dumb Chan'?"[39] This interpretation is eminently sensible, but it robs the dictum of much of the piquancy of its paradox. I venture to suggest another interpretation: "Without attaching [*zhuo*] a single word (to any particular object), one can fully capture the dynamic force of nature (as a whole)."[40] Whether this rendering is acceptable or not, let us now consider the whole poem, of which the dictum is the opening:

Without attaching a single word,
Fully capture the "wind-flow."
Words that do not touch distress
Already carry unbearable grief.
Herein is something truly in control:
With it sink or swim!
Like straining wine till the cup is full,
Or turning back the blossoming season to autumn.
Far-reaching: dust in the air;
Sudden and transient: foam on the sea.
Shallow or deep, gathering or scattering,
Ten thousand takings come to one close.[41]

The first two lines have been fully discussed. For lines three and four, I have adopted the varient reading *yu bu she nan / yi bu kan you* (as translated above) instead of *yu bu she ji / ruo bu kan you* ("Words that do not touch oneself / Seem to carry unbearable grief"),[42] because the former reading is more relevant to the theme of this poem: without explicitly speaking of distress, one can suggest unbearable grief. Line five alludes to the *Zhuang Zi*: "There seems to be something truly in control; it is just that we do not see signs of it."[43] In the present context, "something in control" seems to refer to intuition, by which the writer should sink or swim. In other words, one should rely on intuition rather than technique. Lines seven and eight, as suggested by Guo Shaoyu and Zu Baoquan, are examples of "reserve": when straining out wine, even when the cup is full, one still leaves something behind in the strainer, and when flowers are prevented from full blossoming by a return of autumn chill, some of the beauty is kept back. Following Guo's commentary, we may interpret the last four lines as follows: Dust in the air stretches far, while foam on the sea lasts only for a brief moment. Although such phenomena may differ from each other in being shallow or deep, gathering or scattering, they all follow the same principle. One may consider ten thousand things, but they all rest in one thing, *reserve*.[44]

That Sikong Tu is speaking of capturing the dynamic force of nature through intuition may be corroborated by lines from another poem in the sequence "Embodying and Describing" (*Xingrong*).

> The changing appearances of wind-swept clouds,
> The quintessential spirit of flowers and plants,
> The waves and billows of the sea,
> The rugged crags of mountains—
> All these resemble the great Dao:
> Indentify with them intuitively, even to the dust.
> Leave forms behind but catch true likeness,
> Then you will come close to being the right one.[45]

Admittedly, these lines are also obscure and can be interpreted in many different ways, but there can be little doubt that Sikong advocated capturing the moving spirit of nature with as few words as possible, instead of describing individual objects in concrete detail. To him, "true likeness" resides in capturing the spirit, not in outward verisimilitude.

As mentioned in the preceding chapter, Sikong Tu also advocated "flavor beyond saltiness and sourness," an aesthetic concept that, together with the dictum discussed above, exerted profound influence on later poets and critics. Such influence can be seen in the works of various poets and critics of the Song period (960–1279). Mei Yaochen (1002–1060), in professing that his poetry aimed at "blandness" (*dan*, a term that, as Jonathan Chaves has noted, carries various Daoist connotations),[46] and Ouyang Xiu (1007–1072), in comparing Mei's poetry to the taste of the olive,[47] both echo Sikong Tu's idea of "flavor beyond saltiness and sourness." Furthermore, Mei's remark, recorded by Ouyang, that a poet should "imply endless meaning that is seen beyond words," is consistent with Sikong's dictum, though put in a less drastic way.[48] To be sure, Mei's remark is not entirely original, but it "immediately entered the repertoire of critical formulae" at the time, as Chaves put it.[49]

It is well known that Song poetics was much influenced by Chan.[50] One of the first Song poet-critics to compare poetry to Chan was Li Zhiyi (ca. 1040–ca. 1105), who wrote the following in his poem "Presented to the Reverend Master Xiangying":

> To obtain a line is like obtaining immortality;
> To be enlightened about writing is like being
>     enlightened in Chan.[51]

We may note in passing that, like many other poets, Li uses Daoist and Buddhist terms rather indiscriminately: in the first line he uses the Daoist term for "immortal" (*xian*), while in the second line he explicitly mentions Chan. In his letter to Li Quyan, Li Zhiyi asserts, "There is basically no difference between expounding Chan and writing poetry."[52]

Li's attitude was shared by his contemporary Huang Tingjian (1045–1105), considered the patriarch of the Jiangxi school of poets. Huang's poetics differs from previous poetics of paradox in that he emphasizes conscious artistry and imitation of earlier poets as well as intuition. However, insofar as he recommends conciseness and concentration on single words, he is following the tradition of Sikong Tu. In one of his poems presented to Gao Zimian, Huang writes,

> In a line by the Admonisher [Du Fu], there is an "eye";
> The intent of [the magistrate of] Pengze [Tao Qian] lies
>     in the stringless [zither].[53]

The first line, asserting that a line by Du Fu contains an "eye," or key word, that catches the eye of the reader, may seem to contradict Sikong Tu's dictum, but it is really a modification of it, since one cannot literally refrain from attaching (or putting down) a single word. Huang's thought may be rephrased: "By attaching (putting down) a single word, one may fully capture the 'wind-flow.' " In other words, by concentrating on a single key word, one may achieve maximal effect. The second line reaffirms the ideal of soundless music or wordless poetry [an impossible ideal that can be approached but never reached through such devices as conciseness and understatement]. The two lines, therefore, do not form a contrast, as Adele Rickett thinks,[54] but are really two sides of the same coin. [The "pure poetry" of "eyes" (key words) can express the inexpressible and hint at the ideal of silence that lies beyond words themselves.] Huang's poetics, then, may be considered a practical application of Sikong Tu's dictum rather than a repudiation of it.

Among poet-critics influenced by Chan, Yang Wanli (1127–1206) went one step further than his predecessors who advocated forgetting words after obtaining the meaning. Yang advocated forgetting both words and meaning, while retaining only the "flavor" of poetry. In his preface to a friend's collected poems, Yang writes with a typical semifacetiousness.

> Now, what is poetry all about? [You may say,] "Esteem its words; that is all." But I say, "One who is good at poetry gets rid of words." "If so, then, esteem its meaning; that is all." I say, "One who is good at poetry gets rid of the meaning." "If so, then, having got rid of the words and the meaning, where would poetry exist?" I say, "Having got rid of the words and the meaning, then poetry has somewhere to exist." "If so, then, where does poetry really exist?" I say, "Have you ever tasted candy and tea? Who is not fond of candy? At first it is sweet, but in the end it turns sour. As for tea, people complain of its bitterness, but before its bitterness is over, one is overcome by its sweetness. Poetry is also like this; that is all."[55]

It is interesting that Yang, somewhat in the manner of Chan masters and of the poets Wang Wei and Li Bai, does not answer the last question from his imaginary interlocutor squarely but asks a rhetorical question instead. His comparison of poetry to tea is reminiscent of Ouyang Xiu's comparison of Mei Yaochen's poetry to the taste of the olive, not to mention Lu Ji's "lingering taste of the 'supreme broth,' " Sikong Tu's "flavor beyond saltiness and sourness," and Mei Yaochen's "blandness." However, by adding the ideal of the flavor of poetry beyond both words and meaning to those of the music beyond the strings, the flavor beyond saltiness and sourness, and the meaning beyond words, Yang Wanli made a significant contribution to a synesthetic aesthetics of paradox, which goes beyond the poetics of paradox based solely on the paradox of language.

Significant contributions to the poetics of paradox were also made by Jiang Kui, whose awareness of the metaparadox of poetics I discussed in the previous chapter. In his discourse on poetry, Jiang sums up the poetics of paradox in one short paragraph. "Literature [*wen*] achieves artistry by means of words [*wen*] but does not achieve marvelousness by means of words. Yet without words there can be no marvelousness."[56] He distinguishes four kinds of "lofty marvelousness" (*gaomiao*).

> Poetry has four kinds of lofty marvelousness. The first kind is called "lofty marvelousness of reasoning"; the second is called "lofty marvelousness of idea"; the third is called "lofty marvelousness of imagination"; the fourth is called "lofty marvelousness of spontaneity." What seems obstructed but really flows through is called "lofty marvelousness of reasoning"; what emerges beyond one's expectations is called "lofty marvelousness of idea"; to depict what is hidden and subtle so that it appears like a clear pool which one can see through to the bottom is called "lofty marvelousness of imagination"; what is neither strange nor bizarre, with its colorful decorations peeled off, so that one knows it is marvelous but not wherefore it is marvelous, is called "lofty marvelousness of spontaneity."[57]

These four kinds of marvelousness appear to be arranged in a hierarchical order, from the most rational to the most intuitive. The first kind, which has been identified by Zhang Jian with "paradox," pertains to ingenious reasoning.[58] The second kind involves the conception of surprising ideas and requires inventive thinking rather than logical skill. The third kind requires imagination and descriptive power to make the abstruse manifest. The fourth kind, which is apparently the highest kind, relies on spontaneous intuition; it is free from traces of conscious artistry and defies rational explanation or description.

Jiang Kui also distinguishes four kinds of poetic closure (to use Barbara Herrnstein Smith's term, which has become common currency in critical vocabulary).[59]

A poem depends entirely on the last line; this is like stopping a galloping horse. When both the meaning and the words come to an end, it is like "overlooking the water to see off someone going home"; when the meaning comes to an end but the words do not, it is like "spiraling with a whirlwind"; when the words come to an end but the meaning does not, it is like the returning boat on the Shan stream; when both the words and the meaning have no ending, it is like [meeting] Wenbo Xuezi. What I call "both the words and the meaning coming to an end" refers to cutting off words that might have come later in the middle of their rapid current; it does not mean that one's words as such are exhausted or that one's ideas are really depleted. What I call "the meaning coming to an end but the words not ending" refers to the meaning ending when it should not yet end, so that words need not come to an end; it does not refer to padding with long-winded words. As for "the words coming to an end but the meaning not ending," this does not mean leaving some meaning out, for the meaning is already somewhat discernible in the words. "Both the words and the meaning having no ending" refers to deeply exhausting the meaning in nonending.[60]

This passage is rather obscure, for two reasons. First, the word *jin*, as pointed out in chapter 1, can be taken in the positive sense of "fully express" or "exhaustively describe," or in the negative sense of "exhausted" or "depleted," or even in the neutral sense of "coming to an end" or simply "stopping." Second, it is not clear whether the various allusions involved are *examples* of the four kinds of poetic closure or *metaphors* for them. On the whole, I think the latter is the case, since none of the lines quoted or texts alluded to actually involves the ending of a poem and since the third allusion is to an anecdote in prose and not to a poem at all. I shall now attempt to interpret this passage.

The four kinds of poetic closure appear to be arranged in a hierarchical order, although Jiang does not explicitly correlate them with his four kinds of lofty marvelousness. In the case of the first kind of closure, both the words and the meaning come to an end, which is illustrated by the partial quotation of the line from Song Yu's "Nine Arguments" that Jiaoran quoted as an example of fourfold meaning.[61] The quotation seems to illustrate metaphorically the kind of ending by which the author has fully expressed what he intends to say and leaves nothing to the reader's imagination. The author, however, has not thereby exhausted his vocabulary or depleted his thoughts. In the case of the second kind of closure, the meaning comes to an end but the words do not, a situation that Jiang compares to the fabulous Peng bird "spiraling with the whirlwind" mentioned in the opening passage of the *Zhuang Zi*.[62] Here the author apparently holds something back so as to allow more words to come, but these words are not mere padding. [It might also mean that, although the author has expressed the meaning fully with the words he has chosen, other words might also have been used, and the meaning as such allows for an infinitely rich potential verbal expression.]

In the third case, the words come to an end, but the meaning does not, which is like the returning boat on the Shan stream. In this story, Wang Huizhi (d. A.D. 388) sailed on this stream on a snowy night to visit his friend Dai Kui. On reaching Dai's door, however, Wang turned back without seeing him. When asked why, Wang replied: "I went when in the mood, and when the mood was gone, I returned. Why must I have seen him?"[63] Applied to poetry, this illustration suggests that, if the mood is implied by the words already used, there is no need for more words. In the last case, both the words and the meaning have no ending, which is compared to the parable about Wenbo Xuezi in the *Zhuang Zi*.[64] The fictional Confucius saw Wenbo Xuezi but did not speak to him, whereupon his disciple Zilu asked: "You, Master, have long wished to see Wenbo Xuezi, but when you saw him, you did not speak. Why is that?" Confucius replied, "With someone like this, when you see him with your eyes, there the Dao is, and there can be no room for sound." In poetry, in other words, one can suggest endless meaning by not saying anything. In this last sentence, Jiang again plays on the different meanings of the word *jin*: by not exhausting (*jin*) all available words, one can fully express (*jin*) one's meaning and even suggest meaning without end (*bujin*).

The Song era critic who exerted the greatest influence on later critics and also suffered the most virulent attacks was Yan Yu (ca. 1195–ca. 1245). [Although, as Guo Shaoyu has pointed out, Yan was not at all the first to discuss poetry in terms of Chan or the first to advocate poetry with limited words but unlimited meaning, the great influence of his criticism ensured that certain ideas about poetry associated with Chan, which had become commonplace during the Song era, remained extremely influential throughout later Chinese criticism, when Yan was often regarded as the major spokesperson for a "Chan poetics."][65] I have discussed Yan's theory of poetry elsewhere, but in order to show its relevence to the poetics of paradox, it is necessary to quote once more a crucial passage from his *Canglang's Remarks on Poetry* (*Canglang shihua*), one of the few comprehensive and systematic treatises on poetry in Chinese [and certainly the most important in the tradition after Liu Xie's *Wenxin diaolong*].

> Now, poetry involves a separate kind of talent, which is not concerned with books; poetry involves a separate kind of meaning [or interest, *qu*], which is not concerned with reason [or principles, *li*]. Yet unless one reads widely and investigates principles

exhaustively, one will not be able to reach its ultimate. What is called "not touching the path of reason nor falling into the trap of words" is superior. Poetry is what sings of one's emotion and nature. The masters of the High Tang [eighth century] relied solely on inspired mood (xingqu), like the antelope that hangs by its horns, leaving no traces to be found. Therefore, the miraculousness of their poetry lies in its transparent luminosity, which is not something that one can piece together: it is like sound in the air, color in appearance, the moon in water, or an image in the mirror; the words have an end, but the meaning is inexhaustible.[66]

Sentences from this passage have been quoted innumerable times by both Yan Yu's followers and his detractors, some of whom have, willfully or unwittingly, misrepresented what he wrote. For instance, some critics have quoted the first sentence to show that Yan was against book learning but failed to quote the sentence that immediately follows. Others have taken Yan to task for equating poetry with Chan or for allegedly misunderstanding Chan.[67] Actually, Yan said explicitly that he was using Chan as an analogy for poetry [a comparison that had become commonplace during the later Song era] and never said that they were identical.[68] [Instead, he thought they were similar in some ways, and, as he put it, "discussing poetry is like (ru) discussing Chan."[69] Although Yan's understanding of the history and thought of Chan seems to have been incomplete and inaccurate at times, he probably had as good a grasp of it as did most literati of his day, and his general knowledge of Chan was certainly sufficient to construct a valid analogy with poetry; the allegations made by later detractors that his misunderstanding of Chan was such that the analogy itself must be invalid can be refuted.][70] In any case, we are concerned not with Yan's understanding of Chan but with his contributions to the poetics of paradox.

In the passage quoted above, Yan makes three important points about the poetics of paradox. First, poetry is not concerned with rational knowledge, which is the focus of nonpoetic writings, yet such knowledge is helpful [and even in-dispensable, seemingly, as a prerequisite for achieving the very best in poetry]. Second, ideal poetry suggests infinite meaning or mood beyond words. Third, the best poetry appears effortless and spontaneous, with no trace of conscious artistry. It is noteworthy that Yan sees poetry as different in its *concern* from nonpoetic writing, not in its *structure*, which shows [here at least] that he was not [looking at poetry as] a structuralist or formalist [might have looked at it]. The third point involves the paradox that perfect art is artless, which we have considered in the preceding chapter. Viewed in the light of this paradox, Yan's seeming self-contradiction of advocating, on the one hand, intuitive apprehension or "miraculous awakening" (*miaowu*) and, on the other hand, emulating or learning from (*xue*) the ancients can be resolved. To Yan, "learning from the ancients" does not mean a mechanical process of imitation but an intersubjective experience of "communing with" [or "penetrating to the truth of"] (*can*, a term borrowed from Chan) them, so that one identifies with them and assimilates their art, which then becomes second nature. Thus, there is really no contradiction between intuition and learning, between spontaneity and art.[71]

[Views similar to those of Yan Yu appeared roughly at the same time in the north, in that part of China controlled by the Jin (Jürched, 1115–1234) dynasty. Since it is extremely unlikely that Yan's treatise on poetry was known there, it appears that both Yan and these northern poet-critics were common heirs to various theoretical and critical trends that had begun before 1127, when the empire was still united.[72] After reunification under the Mongols, various critics of the Yuan dynasty (1279–1368) also held similar views, though by this time there may have been direct influence by Yan on them.] Wang Ruoxu (1174–1234), for example, agreed with Yan that great art is artless. "If one takes artistry as artistry, then the artistry will not be sufficient. When artistry and awkwardness complement each other, then people will not get tired. Only those with the utmost artistry can produce artistry from awkwardness."[73] Ultimately, this idea is derived from Lao Zi's saying, "Great artistry seems to be awkwardness."[74]

Yuan Haowen (1190–1257) expresses a similar idea in his "Introduction to the Study of Du Fu's Poetry" (*Du shi xue yin*). "I have presumed to say that the marvelousness of Zimei's [Du Fu's] poetry lies in nothing but what the Buddhists call 'learning until one reaches the state of being without learning.'"[75] All these paradoxes—music without sound, poetry without words, flavor without flavor, end without end, art without art, and learning without learning—are variations on the same theme, and all can be traced back to Lao Zi and Zhuang Zi, with their paradoxical views not only on language but on all human culture.

Wu Cheng (1249–1333), in his "Preface to the Poems of He Youwen," expresses the ideal of "flavor beyond words and meaning" in a somewhat different way: "In poetry, we value that which has its shadow and its spirit but not its form. In He Youwen's poetry, there are no sluggish lines in the poem and no vulgar words in the line. The mechanism is smooth and the sound is clear. Although he has not left form behind, he has already shown formlessness in form. He may indeed be called an able poet."[76] The trinity "form," "shadow," and "spirit" is derived from a poem by Tao Qian entitled "Form, Shadow, and Spirit".[77] Applied here to poetry, "form" refers to the linguistic structure, "shadow" to the meaning, and "spirit" to the supralinguistic dimension of poetry, whether one calls it spirit, mood, flavor, or anything else.

Certain ideas of Yan Yu are echoed by Zhang Zhu (1285–1364) in his "Preface to the *Noon-Stream Collection* [of Chen Yi]" (*Wuxi ji xu*).

When I learned to write poetry in my early years, I took all the works of the ancients and the moderns and read them, and felt as if I had obtained release within. I then realized that what is Heaven-given in one's nature and emotions and what is Heaven-given in sound and music issue forth in words and cannot be casually and easily described. However, one also needs to follow previous writers in order to widen one's knowledge, and to travel in all directions in order to be familiar with the ways of the world. One must make events, objects, feelings, and scenes blend, melt, and become an integral whole, for only then can one peek into the inner chamber of a master of poetry. No doubt here is something of which the changes seem to have a limit but are inexhaustible, the spirit seems to depart but is continuous, and the meaning seems to have been reached and the words seem to have been exhausted but the music lingers on.[78]

The ideas that one needs learning but should not be enslaved by it, that poetry is holistic, and that one should aim at something beyond words were all said earlier by Yan Yu.

The archaists of the Ming dynasty (1368–1644) were all influenced by Yan Yu, although they sometimes disagreed among themselves.[79] We have seen, in the previous chapter, how He Jingming and Li Mengyang disagreed about whether one should discard the ancients as models after reaching poetic enlightenment. We may now consider Xie Zhen (1495–1575), a later archaist who emphasized intuition more than learning from the ancients. Following Sikong Tu and Yan Yu, Xie advocated "flavor" (*wei*) and "inspired mood" (*qu*), such as in the following passage from his *Siming's Remarks on Poetry* (*Siming shihua*):

> [Monk] Guanxiu wrote,
>> Flowers in the courtyard dim and drizzling, the water cool and clear;
>> The child cries and demands the oriole on the tree.

The scene is real, but there is no inspired mood.
Taibai [Li Bai] wrote,

> Snowflakes on Mount Yan as big as mats:
> One by one, blown and fallen on Xuanyuan Tower.

The scene is illusory, but there is flavor.[80]

Furthermore, Xie Zhen distinguishes two kinds of meaning. "In poetry, there is meaning before words and there is meaning after words. The Tang poets had both, [so their poetry] is oblique and flavorful, holistic and traceless. The Song poets always decided on the meaning first, and touched the path of reason, [so their poetry] is rather lacking in the natural order of [intuitive] thought.[81]

In condemning the Song poets for "touching the path of reason," Xie Zhen is of course echoing Yan Yu's remark that the best poetry "does not touch the path of reason." The expression *sizhi*, here translated "the natural order of [intuitive] thought," is taken from the "Intuitive Thought" (*Shensi*) chapter of Liu Xie's *The Literary Mind*.[82] Although Xie Zhen does not explicitly mention intuition, the context in Liu's work provides the justification for my translation here. In another passage, Xie Zhen elaborates on what he means by "meaning before words" and "meaning after words."

Nowadays, when people write poetry, they suddenly set up so many big ideas, and if they restrain them within the lines, then they are in straits: the words will not be able to communicate ideas, and the meaning will not be fully comprehensible. It is like drilling a pool to store the blue sky, in which case one will not be able to get much, or lifting one's cup to collect sweet dew, in which case it will not spread and moisten things widely. This is because what comes out from within is limited, and this is what is called "meaning before words." But sometimes, when one cannot complete a line, one should not let one's thought be worn out, but should read a book to awaken one's mind; then one may suddenly get something: ideas will arise following one's writing brush, and inspiration cannot be checked, which will enter the realm of spiritual transformations, far beyond the reach of deliberate pondering. Or sometimes one may get a whole line because of a word, or complete a line because of a rhyme, all naturally and spontaneously, so that the line and the meaning are both beautiful. It is like joining bamboo pipes together to lead water from a fountain, so that the gurgling sound will fill one's ear, or climbing the city wall to look at the sea, so that the vast rolling waves will fill one's eye. This is because what comes from without is inexhaustible, and this is what is called "meaning after words."[83]

Some of the ideas in this passage may have been inspired by the great Song dynasty poet Su Shi (1037–1101), who once wrote,

> If, in writing poetry, you insist it must be *this* poem,
> Then certainly you are not one who understands poetry.[84]

Su and Xie mean, I believe, that, if poets know exactly what they are going to say before writing a poem, they are not true poets, those who understand the dialectical relationship between language and thought. If poets have definite preconceived ideas about what meaning a poem is to yield, the meaning will at best be what is explicitly stated. If, on the other hand, they allow the words to lead them on and bend to the exigencies of meter, rhyme, and other technical and linguistic considerations, these elements may suggest endless meanings of which the poets may not have been fully aware.

Su Shi's and Xie Zhen's insights into the dialectical relationship between language and thought, between the poetic medium and the creative process, anticipated similar insights on the part of such modern Western poets as Paul Valéry and W. H. Auden. Valéry wrote, "It can happen, then, that the germ is no more than a word or a fragment of a sentence, a line that seeks and toils to create its own justification and so gives rise to a context, a subject, a man, etc."[85] This comment is remarkably similar to Xie Zhen's remarks quoted above. Auden wrote: "A poet has to woo, not only his own Muse, but also Dame Philology, and, for the beginner, the latter is the more important. As a rule, the sign that a beginner has a genuine talent is that he is more interested in playing with words than in saying something original; his attitude is that of the old lady, quoted by E. M. Forster—'How can I know what I think till I see what I say?' "[86] The last remark aptly describes the experience of many poets and may serve as a commentary on Su Shi's lines.

The Ming individualists who opposed archaism did not see language in a paradoxical light, as did many of the archaists. As we have seen in the preceding chapter, Yuan Zongdao betrayed possible signs of logocentrism. However, these individualists were much more interested in *qu*, which, as used by them, does not quite mean "inspired mood" but something like "gusto." The two concepts of *qu* overlap to the extent that both are supposed to be indescribable in words. Yuan Zongdao's younger brother Yuan Hongdao (1568–1610) wrote: "What is rarest in people is gusto, which is like color on mountains, flavor in water, light on flowers, or the airs of a woman. Even someone eloquent cannot say a word about it, and only someone who understands it in his heart knows what it is."[87] A further description of "gusto" is given by Zhao Nanxing (1550–1627) [the great late Ming statesman and literatus, whose views on literature often had a great deal in common with those of the Yuan brothers].

> Now, as for gusto, it is what people have received from Heaven, and cannot be forcibly acquired. Therefore, it is possible to have wide learning but difficult to have ideas; possible to have ideas but difficult to speak; possible to speak but difficult to have flavor; possible to have flavor but difficult to have music; possible to have music but difficult to have airs. When all five are beautiful, we name them [collectively] "gusto." Even the author himself does not know how it comes to be so.[88]

Countless other Ming writers discussed "gusto" and "flavor." Suffice it to say that they all favored some kind of ineffable gusto or taste, which lies beyond words but is suggested by words.

The late Ming and early Qing poet and critic Qian Qianyi (1582–1664), whose advice to a friend to renounce poetry has been quoted in the previous chapter, was a severe critic of Yan Yu,[89] yet he too realized the paradoxical relationship between intuition and learning (*xue*, which means both "study" and "learn from" or "imitate"/"emulate"), as shown in his "Preface to the Collected Works of Master Meicun [Wu Weiye, 1609–1671]."

> In my old age I have entered the Gate of Emptiness [Buddhism], and no longer touch musical sounds [poetry], but have become rather enlightened about the principle of poetry. I consider the way of poetry to be thus: there are those who are capable without studying, and those who are incapable despite studying; there is that which one can study and become capable of by studying, and there is that which one can study but cannot become capable of; there are those who become even more capable by studying, and those who, the more they study, become the more incapable; there is Heaven-given artistry, and there is human effort. If one knows wherefore this is so, then one may come close to poetry and study [how to write] it.[90]

In short, some poetry is the result of spontaneous expression that owes nothing to study, but in most cases natural talent needs to be enriched by study. However, without natural talent, no matter how hard one studies, one will not succeed as a poet. These ideas may not be original, but they are based on lifetime experience and confirm what previous poet-critics have said.[91]

During the Qing period (1644–1912), the poetics of paradox continued to be espoused by some critics. The early Qing philosopher, literatus, and critic Wang Fuzhi (1619–1692), perhaps under the influence of Xie Zhen, discussed "meaning before words" and "meaning after words." "In 'Pick, pick the plantain,' the meaning lies before the words and also after the words, leisurely and poignant, spontaneously producing its atmosphere. Even among pentasyllabic verses, some of the 'Nineteen Poems' still captured this idea. Magistrate Tao [Qian] could somewhat approach this. After that, it became extinct."[92] Wang's choice of the "Pick the plantain" poem from the *Book of Poetry* is somewhat surprising,[93] since this is a simple song sung by women picking the plantain (which may have been believed to bestow fertility),[94] but perhaps the poem's simplicity lends itself to different interpretations, so that it can be said to contain "meaning after words." The choice of the "Nineteen Ancient Poems" and of Tao Qian confirms the impression that Wang Fuzhi favors poetry that is terse and suggestive.

In another passage, Wang Fuzhi shows his preference for suggestiveness over descriptiveness by drawing an analogy between poetry and painting.

> Those who discuss painting say that within the distance of a foot there can be the sweep of ten thousand *li*. One should pay special attention to the word "sweep." If one disregards "sweep," then shrinking ten thousand *li* to one foot would just result in something like a map of the world that appears at the front of *A Comprehensive Account of the Earth*.[95] In writing pentasyllabic quatrains, this is the first principle that one should hold while settling one's thought. Only the High Tang poets captured this marvelousness, such as in:
>
>> Where, sir, is your home?
>> I live by Level Dyke.
>> Let me stop my boat and ask you for a moment:
>> Perhaps we come from the same town?[96]
>
> Where the spirit of the ink shoots out, it reaches the extremities of the four directions without being exhausted. Where there are no words, the meaning is everywhere.[97]

The word translated as "sweep" above is *shi*, which can mean "force," "influence," "prevailing situation," or "general appearance," but here it refers to the sweeping force of a landscape painting, which enables viewers to feel as if they were facing the sweeping prospect of ten thousand *li*. By analogy, the kind of poetry that Wang Fuzhi admires has a sweeping force that suggests endless meanings far beyond what is said. The choice of the quatrain by Cui Hao (d. 754), put in the mouth of a young woman who is obviously attracted to a man she has encountered by chance, is again somewhat surprising. Perhaps Wang chose this poem because the vignette it presents is fraught with dramatic possibilities and readers are free to imagine what consequences this chance encounter may lead to.

Wang Shizhen (1634–1711), whose acceptance of the meta-paradox of poetry was examined in chapter 2, advocated the theory of "spirit and tone" (*shenyun*), which, as I have pointed out elsewhere and as Richard John Lynn has demonstrated in much greater detail, involves capturing the "spirit" of things, mastering the poetic medium, and developing a personal "tone."[98] The kind of poetry that Wang Shizhen espoused does not directly express the poet's own personality but embodies reality as filtered through an individual sensibility. Yet this kind of poetry is not entirely impersonal, for it conveys a personal vision and has a personal tone. Thus, the theory of "spirit and tone" may be paraphrased as the theory of personal impersonality or impersonal personality, another dimension of the poetics of paradox.

Let us now consider the views of an opponent to the poetics of paradox, the eccentric painter and poet Zheng Xie (better known as Zheng Bangqiao, 1693–1765), and see how even he could not completely escape from its influence. In a letter to his younger brother, Zheng wrote:

In literary compositions, the utmost lies in what is "deeply manifesting and thoroughly satisfying," such as the *Zuo* [*Zuozhuan* (Zuo's commentary on the spring and autumn annals)], the *Shi* [*Shiji* (Records of the historiographer), by Sima Qian], the *Zhuang* [*Zi*], the *Sao* [*Lisao* (Encountering sorrow), by Qu Yuan], the poetry of Du [Fu], and the prose of Han [Han Yu, 768–824]. Occasionally these writers may have one or two words not quite finished, or meanings that lie beyond words, which with so little surpass so much. These are their minor good points, like twigs or joints of bamboo, and do not indicate the basic nature of these six gentlemen. But the constrained and petty men of the world take these things alone as [literary] ability and say that in literary compositions one may not let out the secret and should not speak fully, so much that they abuse others as "gabbling on and on without stop." Now, what is called "gabbling on and on without stop" refers to profitless words or "talking about three things without hitting two," that is all. As for expounding the tasks of emperors and kings, or singing of the labors and hardships of the common people, or analyzing and clarifying the subtle principles of the sages and wise men, or depicting the airs and manners of heroes: how could these be done with one or two words? How could those who believe in words beyond words or flavor beyond flavor be able to hold the writing brush and describe it thoroughly? I know that such people will be dazzled in the eye and confused in the mind, turn things upside down and drag them about, and not know where to put their hands and feet. The poetry of Wang [Wei] and Meng [Meng Haoran, 689–740] basically has some solid qualities that cannot be worn away; it is only because they aimed at cultivated purity [i.e. selfless otherworldliness] that they could not reach the depths of Li [Bai] and Du [Fu]. Sikong Biaosheng [Sikong Tu], who thought he had obtained the flavor beyond flavor, is one or two degrees below Wang and Meng. As for the petty men of today, who are a million times inferior to Wang, Meng, and Sikong but take solely "what lies beyond meaning and beyond words" as a means to cover up their own paltriness, they are laughable. When it comes to writing quatrains or "little airs" [xiaoling] in lyric meters, then one must try to surpass others by what lies beyond meaning in words.[99]

It is ironic that, in attacking the followers of Yan Yu, Zheng should be borrowing a phrase from Yan, who wrote, "There are two general kinds of poetry: the one is called 'freely wandering without being hurried [congrong bupo]' and the other is called 'deeply manifesting and thoroughly satisfying [chenzhuo tongkuai].' "[100] Yan's remark, made without explanation, is admittedly rather vague. However, he evidently acknowledges that there are two kinds of poetic excellence: free, spontaneous, and leisurely, or unreservedly expressive and totally satisfying. In this way, he seems to have forestalled later critics who objected to his advocating meaning beyond words [which seems to apply only to the first kind of poetry but not the second; this is the distinction that Zheng himself seems to be making here]. Even more ironic and paradoxical, Zheng Xie, after delivering a diatribe against those who believed in meaning beyond words, admitted that for some short verse forms it is actually necessary to aim at meaning beyond words.

So far we have been concerned with poetry in regular meters [or classical verse] (*shi*). Actually, the poetics of paradox also affected poetry in lyric meters (*ci*, abbreviation of *quzi ci*, or "song words," a type of poetry originally written to existing music, usually in lines of unequal but fixed length).[101] For instance, Zhang Yan (1248–ca. 1320), in his *Origins of the Lyric* (*Ci yuan*), shows his preference for suggestion over description in a passage entitled "Pure and Ethereal" (*Qingkong*).

Lyrics should be pure and ethereal, not solid and substantial. If pure and ethereal, then they will be archaic, classical, lofty, and outstanding. If solid and substantial, then they will be congealed, dry, obscure, and opaque. The lyrics of Jiang Baishi [Jiang Kui] are like a wild cloud flying alone: whether going or coming, it leaves no trace. The lyrics of Wu Mengchuang [Wu Wenying, 1200–1260] are like a many-storied pavilion decorated with seven kinds of precious stones: it dazzles the eye, but if dismantled, does not form proper pieces or segments. This is the theory of the "pure and ethereal" and the "solid and substantial."[102]

This theory is consistent with Jiang Kui's own views, which we have seen, and also echoes Yan Yu's ideal that poetry should leave no trace of conscious artistry. In the next passage, entitled "Meaning and Mood" (*Yiqu*), Zhang Yan remarks: "In lyrics, the chief concern lies in meaning and mood. One must not follow the tracks and borrow the words or ideas of previous writers."[103] After quoting several lyrics by Su Shi, Wang Anshi (1021–1086), and Jiang Kui, Zhang comments, "In all these lyrics, their purity and ethereality contain meaning and mood, which someone without strength of writing cannot easily reach."[104]

[The *locus classicus* for the term *qingkong* seems to be a poem attributed to Li Bai, in which the following couplet appears:

> I dwell beyond the pure air [*qingkong biao*];
> You reside inside the red dust [*hongai zhong*].[105]

Here the contrast is between living up in the mountains in the pure, clean air and down in the dusty mundane world, with the further implication that the former refers to a detached, pristine, and otherworldly existence and the latter to a life caught up in the snares of ambition, greed, vulgarity, and selfishness. If Zhang had this idea in mind when he used *qingkong* here, "purity" as such could refer to a detached point of view or freedom from the attempt to achieve a calculated effect and from any deliberate posing on the part of the author, and "ethereality" ("airiness") could refer to freedom from such things as ostentatious display, crudity of feeling, or the coarseness inherent in explicitness. In metaphorical terms, this is the difference between the elegant simplicity of the mountain recluse and the vulgar extravagance of the merchant or bureaucrat. Being "simple," a lyric will be rich in suggestion and connotation, and its meaning and mood will find elegant expression, but if it is "extravagant," meaning and mood will be obscured and, ultimately, disintegrate.]

Some later critics of the lyric, probably influenced by Huang Tingjian [and the emphasis he placed on conciseness and individual words], paid special attention to the *mot juste*, but opinions often differed as to when a *mot* is *juste*. A notable, if not notorious, case concerns Song Qi (998–1061), who became so famous for a line he wrote that he acquired a popular nickname based on that line: " 'Red apricot blossoms at the tips of twigs, spring feelings riot' Minister" (*Hongxing zhitou chunyi nao Shangshu*). For his part, Zhang Xian (990–1078) became known as the " 'Clouds break up, the moon comes, flowers play with their shadows' Secretary" (*Yun po yue lai hua nong ying Langzhong*) and also as Zhang Sanying, or "Zhang Three Shadows," because his three most famous lines all contain the word "shadow" (*ying*). However, several critics of the Qing period expressed contrary opinions on the quality of Song Qi's line. For instance, the dramatist and critic Li Yu (1611–1680), styled Liweng, or "The Old Man with the Straw Hat" (not to be confused with Li Yu, or Li Houzhu, the poet and last ruler of the Southern Tang dynasty, 937–978), wrote:

> In polishing lines and smelting words, although we esteem what is novel and extraordinary, it must be something novel yet secure, extraordinary yet sure, and what is "secure and sure" does not lie beyond one word, "reason." If you hope your lines will astonish people, you must first try to make your reason convincing to all. Leaving alone contemporary notables, I shall discuss the ancients. Many ancients excelled in this skill. Among them there is one I admire most wholeheartedly, and that is the "Clouds break up, the moon comes, flowers play with their shadows" Secretary; and there is one who has enjoyed fame for going on to a thousand years but who cannot make this stubborn Old Man with the Straw Hat bend, and that is the "Red apricot blossoms at the tips of twigs, spring feelings riot" Minister. The phraseology of the line "clouds break up, the moon comes, . . ." is extremely sharp and novel, yet it is really within reason. As for suddenly adding the word "riot" to the "red apricot blossoms at the tips of twigs," this word is rather difficult to understand. When people fight and make a noise, it is called "riot." If you say "peach and plum blossoms compete over spring," that does actually happen, but as for "red apricot blossoms riot in spring" [or "cause spring to riot," an alternate possible reading of the line], I have never seen it. If the word "riot" may be used, then the words "brawl," "fight," and "hit" may also be used.[106]

Contrary opinion was voiced by Li Yu's younger contemporary, Liu Tiren. "In 'red blossoms at the tips of twigs, spring feelings riot' the one word 'riot' stands out alone in a thousand ages."[107] On these lines Wang Shizhen commented:

> [That Song Qi was called] the "Red apricot blossoms at the tips of twigs, spring feelings riot" Minister was circulated at the time as a fine story. My friend Gongyong [Liu Tiren] sighed over this line with extreme admiration and considered it to be outstanding in a thousand ages. Actually, it was derived from "warmth makes one aware that the apricot twigs are red" [or "wakened by warmth, apricot twigs turn red"; from a lyric by He Ning, 899–955], preserved in the *Huajian* (Among the flowers) [the first anthology of poetry in lyric meters].[108] Except that, it has the marvelousness of blue pigment [which surpasses] the indigo plant [from which it is made] or ice [which surpasses] water [in coldness].[109]

Yet another opinion was expressed by Shen Qian (1620–1670):

> Neither "red apricot blossoms at the tips of twigs, spring feelings riot" nor "clouds break up, the moon comes, flowers play with their shadows" can compare with [the lines by Li Yu (Houzhu)] "The sound of a few drops of rain restrained by the wind, / Dim and pale moonlight, clouds come and go." I have remarked that although Li Houzhu was inept at ruling over his kingdom, when it comes to lyrics he does not fail to be a sovereign, and he makes one feel that Secretary Zhang and Minister Song are mere office boys.[110]

A later critic, Liu Xizai (1813–1881), reaffirms Song Qi's claim to fame.

> In lyrics, there are lines and words that seem to have "touched and hit" [*chuzhuo*]. This is what is called "extreme smelting is not as good as nonsmelting." Yan Yuanxian's [Yan Shu, 991–1055] two lines, "Nothing to be done about flowers' falling away, / Seeming acquaintances—the swallows coming back," are lines that have "touched and hit."[111] In Song Jingwen's [Song Qi's] "red apricot blossoms at the tips of twigs, spring feelings riot," the word "riot" is a word that has "touched and hit."[112]

What he calls "touch and hit" seems to be a more colloquial expression for Yan Yu's "inspired mood" (*xingqu*) or Wang Shizhen's "inspired encounter" (*xinghui*):[113] at the moment of touch or contact (*chu*) with nature, one may hit (*zhuo*) on the right word, which then appears perfectly natural.

To modern readers, the most familiar comments on Song Qi's and Zhang Xian's famous lines are probably those made by Wang Guowei (1877–1927) in his immensely influential *Remarks on Lyrics in the Human World* (*Renjian cihua*). "In 'red apricot blossoms at the tips of twigs, spring feelings riot,' by putting down one word *nao* ('riot'), [the author] fully brings out its world [*jingjie*]; in 'clouds break up, the moon comes, flowers play with their shadows,' by putting down the one word *nong* ('play with'), [the author] fully brings out its world."[114]

As Adele Rickett has noted, Wang Guowei was probably influenced by Huang Tingjian.[115] However, he must have been aware also of the Qing era critics quoted above, especially Liu Tiren, who not only commented on the two lines in a similar fashion but also anticipated Wang Guowei in the use of the term "world" (*jingjie*) in another passage, albeit casually and not at all as consistently as did Wang.[116]

The tradition of the poetics of paradox has by no means become extinct in China. The idea that poetry should be implicit rather than explicit and that it should suggest meaning beyond words is still held by some Chinese critics and scholars. For instance, Zhu Guangqian (b.1898), the best-known aesthetician in China, wrote in his essay *Wuyan zhi mei* (Beauty without words, or The beauty of nonspeech): "Endless meanings are conveyed by limited words, therefore many meanings all lie in nonspeech. The reason why literature is beautiful does not lie merely in limited words, but even more in endless meanings."[117] Although this essay was first published in 1924, it was reprinted in 1980 and cited by another writer, Zhang Wenxun, in 1983.[118]

I do not claim that the poetics of paradox is uniquely Chinese. Some Western poets and philosophers, for instance, have paid attention to the importance of silence, as the following short survey reveals. The device aposiopesis (stopping suddenly as if unable to proceed) is a kind of poetics of paradox in minature form. Shakespeare pretends that his Muse is tongue-tied and pleads with his love:

> Then others for the breath of words respect,
> Me for my dumb thoughts, speaking in effect.[119]

Here he reminds us of Cao Pi's deliberate inarticulateness, which proved more effective than his brother's eloquence.

Note also the familiar lines from Keats's "Ode on a Grecian Urn."

> Heard melodies are sweet, but those unheard
> Are sweeter.[120]

These words recall Lao Zi's saying "Great music has no sound," as well as Tao Qian's zither without strings and Bai Juyi's line from "The Lute Song" (*Pipa xing*), "at this moment, soundlessness surpasses sound,"[121] even though there is a difference. As Qian Zhongshu pointed out, the Chinese writers were referring to silence in music, whereas Keats alluded to silence in order to reinforce visual perception.[122]

Thomas Carlyle valued silence above speech. "As the Swiss Inscription says: *Sprechen ist silbren Schweigen ist golden* (Speech is silvern, Silence is golden); or, as I might express it, speech is of time, silence is of Eternity."[123]

Paul Valéry would, it seems, have endorsed Yan Yu's ideal of poetry with limited words but unlimited meaning, for he wrote, "Poetry's special aim and own true sphere is the expression of what cannot be expressed in the finite function of words."[124]

Mikel Dufrenne suggested a kind of poetics of paradox when he said: "The less expressive [the writer's] language—

that is to say, the more reticent, more discreet, more imper-sonal—the better he expresses himself."[125]

Maurice Merleau-Ponty repeatedly expressed his paradox-ical view of language versus silence.

> Now if we rid our minds of the idea that our language is the trans-lation or cipher of an original text, we shall see that the idea of *complete* expression is nonsensical, and that all language is indirect or allusive—that is, if you wish, silence. . . .
>
> True speech . . . —speech which signifies, which finally ren-ders *"l'absent de tous les bouquets"* present and frees the meaning captive in the thing—is only silence in respect to empirical usage, for it does not go so far as to become a common name. . . .
>
> But what if language expresses as much by what is between words as by the words themselves? By what it does not "say" as by what it "says"?[126]

And Derrida, with typical aplomb, declares, "We must find a speech that maintains silence."[127]

Finally, the drama critic of the *New York Times*, D.J.R. Bruckner, once remarked of Sam Shepard: "Shepard has a powerful instinct for the effect of silence. Effective silences define the climactic moment in several of his plays."[128]

All of these quotations are examples of individual flashes of insight. The Chinese critics discussed in this chapter, how-ever, contributed consciously to a tradition that dealt broadly with the poetics of paradox.

# 4

## The Paradox
## of Interpretation

The poetics of paradox leads inexorably to the paradox of interpretation. If the true meaning of poetry lies beyond words, then how can one interpret it in words? Yet where can one seek the limitless meaning beyond words if not from the limited words of the text?[1] Thus, Chinese critics who subscribed to the poetics of paradox did not stop interpreting poetry, any more than have such contemporary Western critics as Harold Bloom, who declared, "There are no interpretations but only misinterpretations."[2] Although critics who disbelieve in the possibility of interpretation may treat the texts they interpret as palimpsests, presumably they still wish their own texts to be read and understood rather than misread and misunderstood. Such is the paradox of interpretation.

Furthermore, the Chinese word *jie*, whose primary meaning is "to dissect," also means both "to understand" and "to interpret." It therefore contains within itself the hermeneutic circle in a nutshell and might even suggest that to interpret is to deconstruct. Etymology apart, we may consider how the poetics of paradox in Chinese affected the interpretation of poetry and how some Chinese critics dealt with the problems of interpretation. Since critics must interact with a hermeneutic tradition in which or against which they work, just as poets must interact with a creative tradition in which or against which they work, we need to survey briefly the Confucian hermeneutic tradition in its interpretations of the *Book of Poetry* and subsequent poetry.

One can discern in the Confucian hermeneutic tradition two different, if not opposite, tendencies, which may be termed moralism and intentionalism. The first tendency is exemplified by Confucius himself, who was wont to quote lines from the *Book of Poetry* to illustrate a moral lesson. A Western scholar, Donald Holzman, has accused Confucius of "ruthless misinterpretation,"[3] but I believe it would be truer to say that Confucius was interested not in interpreting the *Book of Poetry* but in borrowing words from it to suit his own purposes. In his time it was common practice (on diplomatic occasions, for instance) to quote from this anthology as an indirect and erudite way of expressing oneself. The lines involved were quoted out of context, which both the quoter and the listener would know, to suit a new context, and nobody pretended that such practice was intended to elucidate the meaning of the original poem.

The most notorious case of Confucius's misinterpretation of the *Book of Poetry* concerns the line *si wu xie*. In the original context, the first syllable is an initial particle without semantic content [a kind of metrical particle or filler word], and the line describes horses running "without deviating" (*wu xie*),[4] but Confucius apparently used the words to mean "thoughts without deviation [evil/depravity]" or "no deviating [evil/depraved] thoughts" when he said, "The three hundred poems [of the *Book of Poetry*] may be summed up in one remark: 'No deviating thoughts.' "[5] Some Chinese scholars have been embarrassed by his seeming failure to recognize a metrical particle, while some Western ones have been shocked by what appears to be a case of deliberate distortion of meaning. I think Confucius indulged in a species of punning: he was using the same words to mean something different, and one need neither be embarrassed nor shocked.

The second tendency in Confucian hermeneutics, intentionalism, was initiated by Mencius, who once remarked:

"One who interprets [the *Book of Poetry*] should not let the words damage the phrases, or the phrases damage the intent [*zhi*]. To encounter [the author's] intent with [one's own] idea [*yi*]: this is the way to get it."[6] The word translated "idea" may also be rendered "mind" or even "imagination." It is not clear what precisely Mencius meant by this word, and the whole remark certainly leaves some room for interpreters to exercise their own wits, although the general drift is to claim the possibility and necessity of recovering authorial intent.

Encouraged by Confucius's example, later Chinese scholars and critics interpreted the poems in the *Book of Poetry* in such a way as to make them yield moral lessons. Such interpretations, which are often far-fetched, have been called by many Western scholars allegorical interpretations. However, as Pauline Yu has demonstrated, these interpretations differ radically from Western allegoresis but rather resemble Dante's tropological level of interpretation: instead of using the particular and concrete to represent the universal and abstract, these interpretations sought to relate each poem to particular historical persons and events.[7] Some later poems were often subjected to the same kind of treatment.

At the same time, Mencius's dictum that one should encounter the author's intent with one's own mind gave critics confidence in claiming to recover what the author intended to mean. The combination of Confucian moralism and Mencian intentionalism led to the historico-biographico-tropological approach, which has remained the dominant mode of literary interpretation in China down to the present day. On the one hand, poems are generally assumed to be biographical, and great pains are taken to pin every poem down to a precise date. On the other hand, when the speaker of a poem is clearly not the historical author, such as when a male poet assumes a female persona, or when a poem appears to be concerned with erotic love, then critics will resort to ingenious and far-fetched interpretations to uncover supposedly hidden references to contemporary political events or to the poet's personal circumstances. In other words, what may be quite innocently love poems or not so innocently symbolic poems are all treated as *poèmes à clef*. However, it must be admitted that some Chinese poets did write and read poems in this manner, and the tropological mode of interpretation cannot be totally ignored.

Despite the dominance of the historico-biographico-tropological mode of interpretation, Chinese critics, with their genius for eclecticism, managed in varying degrees to escape from its limitations. Without openly repudiating Confucian moralism or Mencian intentionalism, they quietly developed other modes of interpretation, which were concerned with neither moralization nor authorial intent but with such linguistic aspects of poetry as prosody and verbal style, or such supralinguistic concepts as "inspired mood," "spirit and tone," and "world," some of which we have seen in chapter 3.

Even orthodox Confucians allowed some flexibility in interpretation. The "Commentary on the Appended Phrases" to the *Book of Changes*, traditionally attributed to Confucius, contains the remark, "When a humane one sees it [the Way], he calls it humane; when a wise one sees it, he calls it wise."[8] Although this aphorism was not concerned with the interpretation of poetry, it was often cited in later writings to justify or reconcile different interpretations of the same poem.

The Confucian scholar Dong Zhongshu (176–104 B.C.) declared: "[The *Book of*] *Poetry* has no general explication [*shi wu da gu*]."[9] The word *da*, which I have translated "general," can also be interpreted as "communicative," and Zhang Longxi has translated the sentence "Poetry has no direct interpretation."[10] His translation may have been influenced by Qian Zhongshu's interpretation of this dictum: "The 'meaning' of poetry is *inexplicit*, and therefore it cannot be understood as soon as it reaches one's eye or be picked up as soon as one holds forth one's fingers; yet the 'meaning' of poetry is *not indeterminate*, and therefore the interpretation cannot change according to the interpreter or the matter in hand (*inexplicit without being indeterminate*) [the words in italics are in English in the original Chinese text]."[11] Whether we take *da* as "direct" or "general" (or "universally applicable"), the fact remains that Dong Zhongshu was trying to justify the Confucian practice of interpreting poetry according to the present occasion [i.e. to use it to bolster a position in moral argumentation—reinterpreting it to serve rhetorical purposes]—a practice that went rather against the Mencian injunction to recover authorial intent. Dong was speaking of the *Book of Poetry*, but his dictum was later applied to poetry in general, as a convenient slogan to invoke when one wanted to justify a new interpretation. However, the dictum was really a double-edged sword: it could be used to justify Confucian moralistic and tropological interpretations, but it could also be used to justify nonmoralistic interpretations.

We may now look at some examples of how certain Chinese poet-critics dealt with problems of interpretation. Tao Qian, in his brief fictionalized autobiography, "The Biography of Master Five-Willows" (*Wuliu Xiansheng zhuan*), describes himself thus: "He is fond of reading books, but does not seek too much understanding [*jie*]. Whenever there is a 'meeting of minds' [*huiyi*], he will be so happy as to forget to eat."[12] The word I translated "meeting of minds" can also be rendered simply "understanding." However, I believe there is a subtle difference between *jie* and *huiyi*: the former refers to rational comprehension attained after analytical interpretation; the latter refers to intuitive apprehension without analysis. The former cannot be achieved without language; the latter need not, and perhaps cannot, be described in words. However, Tao did not totally reject analytical interpretation, for in a poem he describes the pleasure of sharing his love of reading with his neighbors.

> Rare writings together we enjoy;
> Doubtful meanings, together analyze.[13]

The two kinds of understanding complement each other and in fact constitute the hermeneutic circle.

In chapter 3, we noted Mei Yaochen's remark that a poet should "imply endless meaning that is seen beyond words," as recorded by Ouyang Xiu. When the latter asked for examples, Mei replied:

> The author obtains it in his mind, and the reader meets it with his own idea: it is difficult to point at it and describe it in words. However, one can roughly speak of what it is more or less like. Take this couplet by Yan Wei [eighth century]:

> > In the willowy pond, spring water swells;
> > Over the flowery bank, the evening sun lingers.[14]

> Does not the appearance of the sky, the manner of the season—harmonious, mild, relaxed, and leisurely—seem as if it were right before one's eyes? Or take Wen Tingyun's [ca. 812–870]

> > Sound of cockcrow, moon over thatched inn;
> > Someone's footprints, frost on Plank Bridge.[15]

> Or Jia Dao's [777–841]

> > Strange birds cry in the vast wilderness;
> > Setting sun frightens the traveling man.[16]

> Do not the hardships of the road and the detained traveler's sad thoughts appear beyond the words?[17]

Mei's reply is typical of many poet-critics who, when faced with the seemingly impossible task of describing in words the wonders of poetry lying beyond words, resort to quoting lines, especially couplets, as illustrations.[18] This mode of interpretation is not very helpful, but it does give us some idea of what is meant by "meaning beyond words."

Mei Yaochen also provides us with a humorous example of misinterpretation.

There was someone who wrote on the writing of poetry:

> All day long I seek but cannot find it,
> Yet at times it comes of its own accord.

This means that a good line of poetry is hard to get, but an interpreter said, "This is a poem about someone's lost cat!"[19]

The presumably deliberate misinterpretation of the facetious interpreter may be considered a parody of Confucian tropological interpretations.

Xie Zhen, whose ideas about "meaning before words" and "meaning after words" we have seen,[20] also commented briefly on the interpretation of poetry. "In poetry, there is that which can be interpreted or understood [jie], that which cannot be interpreted or understood, and that which need not be interpreted or understood. It is like the moon in water or a flower in the mirror. Don't be bogged down by its traces, and it will be all right."[21]

Xie was criticized by a later scholar, He Wenhuan (late eighteenth century), who remarked:

> In interpreting or understanding poetry, one should not be bogged down [by the literal meaning]. This can be seen from what Confucius said [about the disciples with whom] he could discuss [the Book of] Poetry, and from what Mencius quoted. Yet there is definitely no reason why it cannot be interpreted or understood. Xie Maoqin [Xie Zhen] originated the theory of "there is that which can be interpreted or understood and that which cannot be interpreted or understood" and left behind endless harm.[22]

Here he refers to Confucius's approval of the way in which some of his disciples quoted lines from the Book of Poetry and gave them moralistic interpretations and to Mencius's insistence that one should not adhere to the literal meaning when interpreting texts. He Wenhuan's stricture against Xie seems ill advised, for many other critics, too numerous to mention, often expressed similar ideas when they made such state-

ments as "it lies between what can be interpreted or understood and what cannot be interpreted or understood [*zai kejie
bukejie zhi jian*]," or "it can be met by the mind but cannot be
conveyed in words [*keyi yihui, bukeyi yan zhuan*]." All such
statements bear witness to the paradox of interpretation.

Let us now consider several points at which the concerns
of some traditional Chinese poet-critics and those of some
contemporary Western literary theorists seem to converge,
while noting differences that remain between them. One
possible point of convergence is that between the Chinese
idea of *can* and the phenomenological concept of intersubjectivity. The word *can* was borrowed by poet-critics from Chan
Buddhism. [There it means a number of things, depending
on the context. It can mean, for instance, to participate in
Chan meditation, to study the Way of Chan (seek out a master and inquire about the Way), and also, simply, "to commune with" or "pay homage to."] Applied to poetry, *can shi*
may be interpreted as ["studying the way of poetry,"] "meditation on poetry," as well as "communing with and paying
homage to the poet." That this interpretation is not far-
fetched may be borne out by various lines of poetry by poets
of the Song period cited by Guo Shaoyu.[23] For example, Zeng
Ji (1084–1166) wrote,

> Learning [to write] poetry is like communing in Chan:
> Be careful not to commune with dead lines.[24]

Dai Fugu (dates unknown), a contemporary of Yen Yu,
wrote,

> If you wish to commune with poetic rules,
>     it is like communing in Chan:
> Miraculous taste is not conveyed by words.[25]

And another poet of the same era, Xu Rui, wrote,

> I wish to befriend the ancients,
> Commune with them till I reach wordlessness.[26]

All these lines bear witness to the paradox that, by means of meditating on the words of a poem, one reaches the state of wordless communion with the spirit of the poet.

Yan Yu gave the idea of *can shi* its most eloquent exposition.

> Try to take the poems of the Han and the Wei and thoroughly meditate on/commune with them; next, take the poems of the Jin and the Song and thoroughly meditate on/commune with them; next, take the poems of the Southern and Northern dynasties and thoroughly meditate on/commune with them; next, take the poems of Shen [Quanqi], Song [Zhiwen], Wang [Bo], Yang [Jiong], Lu [Zhaolin], Lo [Binwang], and Admonisher Chen [Zi'ang] [all poets of the early Tang era] and thoroughly meditate on/commune with them; next, take the poems of the various masters of the Kaiyuan and Tianbao periods and thoroughly meditate on/commune with them; next, take only the poems of the two masters Li [Bai] and Du [Fu] and thoroughly meditate on/commune with them; . . . then take all the poems of the various masters of the Late Tang and thoroughly meditate on/commune with them; then take up the poems of the various schools of the present dynasty from Su [Shih] and Huang [Tingjian] down and thoroughly meditate on/commune with them: as to what is truly right and what is truly wrong, there will be that which naturally cannot be concealed. If you still do not see anything therein, then it is because your true judgment has been obscured by "wild fox heterodoxy": you are past remedy and will never have awakening.[27]

As I pointed out before, in this way Yan Yu resolved the seeming contradiction between intuitive apprehension of the way of poetry and learning from the ancients.

The Chinese idea of communing with poetry and the phenomenological concept of intersubjectivity are comparable on two counts. First, both imply that a poem is not a dead object but a living presence, and since different readers may commune with the same poem, the poem becomes an intersubjective intentional object, which is Roman Ingarden's definition of a literary work of art.[28] Second, both the Chinese critics and the phenomenologists assign an active role to the reader, who does not simply allow himself or herself to be affected by the work but actively interacts with it.

Of course, there are significant differences not only between the Chinese critics and the phenomenologists but also among phenomenologists themselves. For instance, whereas the Chinese critics relied on intuition, the phenomenologists employ rational analysis. However, Yan Yu did engage in rational arguments, even though he advocated intuition. Furthermore, both the Chinese critics and Ingarden believe in the accessibility of authorial meaning, whereas to Mikel Dufrenne a work of art is a quasi subject, not an expression of the author's subjectivity. To be more specific, the idea of communing with an ancient poet obviously implies a belief in the accessibility of the author's intended meaning. This Chinese belief is shared by Ingarden, who claims that anyone who understands the linguistic system (Saussure's *langue*) can determine the meaning of the words as intended by the author.[29] On the other hand, Dufrenne's quasi subject refers to the aesthetic object that "bears its meaning within itself and is a world unto itself"[30] and should therefore be distinguished from the author's own lived world (*Lebenswelt*).

Another point of possible convergence between some traditional Chinese poet-critics and some contemporary Western theorists concerns the indeterminacy of meaning and its necessary consequence, pluralism in interpretation. The ideas of "meaning beyond words" and "poetry with limited words but limitless meaning" imply that there can be no single definitive interpretation of a poem and that interpretation is an open-ended process, for the meaning beyond words perceived by each reader cannot be assumed to be identical. Even that perceived by the same reader at different readings cannot be assumed to be identical. The necessity of pluralism was realized by Wang Fuzhi, who wrote: "The author uses consistent thought, and each reader obtains what he can according to his own feeling/nature [*qing*]. . . . The wandering of human feeling/nature is limitless, and each one encounters what he does according to his own feeling/nature."[31]

Furthermore, Chinese critics often modified the saying attributed to Confucius, "When a humane one sees it, he calls it humane; when a wise one sees it, he calls it wise," to read, "A humane one sees humanity; a wise one sees wisdom [*renzhe jian ren zhizhe jian zhi*]," as an explanation, if not justification, for different interpretations. They also frequently quoted Zhuang Zi's comment on disputes among different schools of thought: "That is also a yes-or-no; this is also a yes-or-no [*bi yi yi shifei ci yi yi shifei*]."[32] Such a relativistic attitude allows for an indefinite number of interpretations of the same text.

In contemporary Western literary theory and hermeneutics, indeterminacy is an important and controversial topic. Here I cannot enter into discussions of the many complex issues involved in the controversy concerning determinacy versus indeterminacy but shall focus attention on Roman Ingarden's and Wolfgang Iser's respective conceptions of indeterminacy in literary texts and compare them with some Chinese ideas.

In *The Literary Work of Art* and *The Cognition of the Literary Work of Art*, Ingarden postulates that every literary work of art contains spots or places of indeterminacy, which are filled in by the reader during the process of "concretization." An example he gives of such a place of indeterminacy is the unspecified color of an old man's hair in a story.[33] For Ingarden, the existence of places of indeterminacy accounts for the possibility of an indefinite number of concretizations of the same work.

> In a word, the literary work itself is to be distinguished from its respective concretizations, and not everything that is valid for the concretization of the work is equally valid for the work itself. But the very possibility that one and the same literary work can allow any number of concretizations, which frequently differ signifi-

cantly from the work itself and also, in their content, differ significantly from themselves, has its basis, among other things, in the
schematic structure of the object stratum of a literary work, a
structure which allows spots of indeterminacy.[34]

For those not familiar with Ingarden's terminology, I
should explain that the "object stratum" refers to the stratum
in the structure of a literary work that pertains to "represented objects," such as trees and mountains in a poem or
characters and events in a novel or short story. Since an author cannot exhaust all possible details of any object, places
of indeterminacy are inevitable.

Ingarden's concept of indeterminacy has been ably criticized by Wolfgang Iser, who summed up his critique in these
words:

> There would appear, then, to be two major drawbacks to Ingar-
> den's theory. First, he is unable to accept the possibility that a
> work of art may be concretized in different, equally valid, ways;
> and second, because of this blind spot he overlooks the fact that
> the reception of many works of art would be simply blocked if
> they could only be concretized according to the norms of classical
> aesthetics. However, Ingarden's incontrovertible achievement is
> the fact that, with the idea of concretization, he broke away from
> the traditional view of art as mere representation. With this con-
> cept of concretization he drew attention to the structure condi-
> tioning the reception of the work, even though he did not regard
> the concept primarily as one of communication. For him, concre-
> tization was just the actualization of the potential elements of the
> work—it was not an interaction between text and reader; this is
> why his "places of indeterminacy" lead only to an undynamic
> completion, as opposed to a dynamic process in which the reader
> is made to switch from one textual perspective to another, himself
> establishing the connections between "schematized aspects," and
> in doing so transforming them into a sign-sequence.[35]

To Iser, who believes that "the meaning of a literary text is
not a definable entity but, if anything, a dynamic happen-

ing,"[36] indeterminacy pertains not so much to the text as to the relationship between text and reader.

> As a structure of communication [the literary text] is identical nei-
> ther with the reality it refers to, nor with the disposition of its
> possible recipients, for it virtualizes both the prevailing concepts
> of reality (from which it draws its own repertoire) and the norms
> and values of its prospective readers. And it is precisely because
> it is not identical to world or reader that it is able to communicate.
> The nonidentity manifests itself in degrees of indeterminacy,
> which relate less to the text itself than to the connections estab-
> lished between text and reader during the reading process.[37]

Turning back now to Chinese poetics, we see that, although there is no Chinese equivalent to the term "indeterminacy," the phenomenon is common in Chinese poetry.
Chinese poets often use such general terms as "flower" and
"bird," without specifying the color, shape, size, and so on.
To that extent, Ingarden's phrase "places of indeterminacy"
can apply easily to Chinese poetry. However, there is a basic
difference between Ingarden and the Chinese critics because
of different underlying conceptions of poetry. *Pace* Iser's
claim that Ingarden broke away from the traditional (Western) view of art as mere representation, I think Ingarden did
not free himself entirely from the traditional Western mimetic
concept of art, as I have suggested elsewhere.[38] With reference to the color of the old man's hair mentioned above, Ingarden observed, "Thus, if it is advisable for any aesthetic
reasons, it is more probable and desirable to concretize the
man as having grey hair rather than black hair."[39]

To him, a successful concretization of a literary work depends on the degree to which the concretized work resem-
bles one's experience of the "real" world. In contrast,
Chinese poets and critics, who often had either an [individ-
ualistic and personal] expressive or a [self-transcendent]
"metaphysical" conception of poetry [i.e. literature manifests
or explores the underlying principle, the Dao, of the uni-

verse],[40] were interested not in detailed representations of reality but in capturing the essential "spirit" (*shen*) or "mood" (*qu*) or "tone" (*yun*) of a poetic world, to which particulars are often irrelevant. Of course, when particular details are relevant [to the personal expression or the metaphysical vision], they are specified [but even this feature is played down in the traditions of Chinese poetry that tend to cast such experiences in universal terms].

Iser's conception of indeterminacy is also different from Chinese views. Whereas Iser attributes the cause of indeterminacy to the nonidentity of the text with either the world it refers to or the norms and values of the prospective readers, Chinese critics such as Wang Fuzhi attribute indeterminacy to differences in temperament among readers. It may seem paradoxical that the Chinese, who, according to most Western experts on China, are not prone to individualism, should emphasize differences in individual temperament as a cause of indeterminacy of meaning and plurality of interpretation, whereas modern Western literary theorists, who are presumably steeped in individualism, should attribute indeterminacy of meaning to different mind-sets, or presuppositions, or what Heidegger calls fore-structures,[41] all of which are culture-bound rather than grounded in individual temperament.

This seeming contradiction may be resolved in two ways. First, contrary to what Western experts often assert, there have always been great individualists in China, both among the literati, such as the poets Qu Yuan, Ruan Ji (210–263), Tao Qian, Li Bai, and many others, and among nonliterati, such as the knights-errant Hou Ying (326–257 B.C.), Jing Ke (d. 227 B.C.), and many others.[42] Second, since Chinese poets and readers largely shared a common culture, differences in interpretation could not generally be attributed to different presuppositions about the world but should more likely be attributed to differences in individual temperament.[43] I do not mean to suggest that premodern Chinese poets and readers had identical mind-sets or held identical world views, but only that most of them were eclectic or syncretic in their thinking and would not have found it difficult to deduce what another reader's presuppositions about the world might be. [For instance, during the Song and post-Song times, it was common for someone to combine or synthesize Confucian, Daoist, and Buddhist views. The basic elements so combined or synthesized were limited enough in number and scope that someone combining or synthesizing them differently would still have no difficulty in arriving with a fair degree of accuracy at another's presuppositions.] In contrast, in the contemporary Western world [with its fragmented, diffuse, and pluralistic culture], one can hardly assume what another's presuppositions about the world might be.

It may be helpful to examine indeterminacy in the context of what I discern to be the four phases of understanding, or interpretation—the lexical, the syntactic, the referential, and the intentional—and to consider the interactions among these phases. These four phases are not the same as the four strata of the structure of a literary work of art, described by Ingarden: the four interpretive phases are conceived of as constituting a dynamic process, whereas Ingarden's four strata suggest a static object.

In the *lexical* phase of understanding, meaning is usually determinate. No one who can read English will question the lexical meaning of the words "the fat cat sat on the mat," just as no one who can read classical Chinese will question the lexical meanings of the words *ming yue song jian zhao* ("the bright moon shines among pines"), a line from Wang Wei.[44] Sometimes a word may have several possible meanings, but the verbal context can often, though not always, determine which meaning is the relevant one. For instance, the word "fair" in English can have various meanings: when Faustus addresses Helen, "Thou art fairer than the evening air," the word "fair" means "beautiful"; when the three witches in *Macbeth* intone, "Fair is foul and foul is fair," the word "fair" means "clear" or "sunny"; and when John Donne writes, "I can love both fair and browne," the word "fair" means "blonde."[45] In Chinese, especially in very old texts, the meaning of a word may be indeterminate, even when the verbal context is considered. For example, in the poem "The Quiet Girl" (*Jingnü*) from the *Book of Poetry*, the character *nü* can be taken either as *nü* ("girl") or as a loan for *ru* ("you") in some of the lines, and we can only argue which makes better sense, not which was intended by the author.[46] When several possible meanings of the same word may coexist at the same time and when there is no need to make a choice among alternative meanings, then indeterminacy shades into what William Empson called ambiguity and what W. K. Wimsatt called plurisignation.

In the second phase of understanding or interpretation, the *syntactic*, indeterminacy may also occur. For instance, the English sentence "I saw a man with a telescope" can be interpreted in three ways: "I saw a man who was carrying a telescope," or "Using a telescope, I saw a man," or "I habitually saw a man in half with a telescope."[47] Formerly, I discounted entirely the last alternative, but now I realize that even this interpretation is possible under certain circumstances, as we shall see. In classical Chinese, which is much more flexible than English with regard to syntax, indeterminacy may occur more frequently. Consider the following lines from a famous lyric by Su Shi:

> *Duoqing ying xiao wo*
> Much-feeling should laugh me
> *Zao sheng hua fa*
> Early grow gray hair

Some interpreters take *duoqing* ("[one who has] much feeling") as the subject and read the lines as: "The affectionate one should laugh at me for growing gray hair so early." Others take the first line as an inversion of *ying xiao wo duoqing* ("[People] should laugh at me for being too full of feeling or sentimental").[48] Among those who choose the former interpretation, some have even punctuated the line differently.

> Duoqing ying xiao
> Wo zao sheng hua fa
> [One who has much feeling should laugh:
> I am growing gray hair so early][49]

This example illustrates how the way one construes a sequence of words syntactically may affect one's semantic understanding of the words as well.

Whereas the first two phases of understanding or interpretation are concerned with the linguistic structure of a text, the last two phases are concerned with the imaginary world created by the text. The third, or *referential*, phase differs from the first, or *lexical*, insofar as two or more lexical items may have the same referent, while the same lexical item may have two or more referents. In the well-known English example, "morning star" and "evening star" both refer to the planet Venus.[50] In classical Chinese, the same planet is known as Taibai ("great white") or Jinxing ("metal star"). When it appears in the morning in the east, it is called Qiming ("opening-up brightness"), and when it appears in the evening in the west, it is called Changgeng ("long *geng*"). It should be explained that *geng* is the seventh of the ten "heavenly stems" (*tiangan*), a series of signs in combination with the twelve "earthly branches" (*dizhi*) to designate years, months, days, and (less often) hours. In traditional Chinese cosmology, the sign *geng* corresponds to the direction west, the color white, the season autumn, and the element metal (one of the five elements or agents, *wuxing*, the other four being wood, water, fire, and earth). Since autumn is a time of decay [dynastic decline and political instability?] and metal is used to make weapons, the planet Taibai is said to augur the appearance of a great general. To complicate matters further, there is a mountain called Taibai in North China. Finally, the poet Li Bai, according to his biographers, was given the personal name Bai and the courtesy name Taibai because his mother had dreamed of the planet Taibai when she conceived him.[51] The significance of these possibilities when we encounter the name Taibai in Li Bai's poems will be discussed later.

Meanwhile, let us look at a Chinese word that may have two different referents: *furong*, which may refer to the lotus or the hibiscus. In Wang Wei's quatrain *Xinyi wu* (Magnolia village), the first line reads:

> *Mumo furong hua*
> Treetop *furong* flower[52]

At first sight, *furong* here may seem to refer to the hibiscus, since lotus does not, of course, grow on treetops, and some translators have translated the line accordingly.[53] However, the title should give us pause. Furthermore, as commentators have pointed out, Wang Wei is alluding to a line from the *Xiang jun* (which some scholars take as "The Lord of the River Xiang" and others as "The Princess of the River Xiang," one of a group of shamanistic songs of the third century B.C.).

> *Xian furong xi mumo*
> Pluck lotus oh treetop[54]

In the original line, the speaker compares his or her futile efforts to win the diety's love to the attempt to pluck lotus flowers from treetops, but in Wang Wei's poem the allusion is turned upside down: the speaker pretends to exclaim, "Look, lotus flowers on treetops!"—as if by some miracle lotus were blossoming on treetops, when in fact these are magnolia flowers, as indicated by the title. That Wang Wei is indeed writing about magnolia flowers and not lotus or hibiscus is corroborated by his friend Pei Di's accompanying poem, which contains the lines:

> *Kuang you xinyi hua*
> Moreover have magnolia flower
> *Se yu furong luan*
> Color with lotus confuse[55]
> [Moreover there are the magnolia blossoms,
> The color confused with that of the lotus.]

Although the verbal context, including the title of a poem, can generally determine the referent, indeterminacy in the referential phase is always a possibility, since, as mentioned above, no writer can exhaust all possible details about any object, and some details are bound to be left unspecified. In Chinese poetry, unspecified details are usually irrelevant to the essential mood or main intent of the poem, which pertains to the last phase.

The last phase of understanding or interpretation, the *intentional*, is the most controversial. Without siding with intentionalists or anti-intentionalists, we may attempt to clarify the issue by keeping in mind the distinction between the intrinsic intention of the text and the extrinsic intention of the author. The former refers to the main thrust of the text or *what* it points to, the latter refers to the author's motive in writing, or *why* he wrote what he did.[56] The intrinsic intention can usually be inferred from the text itself. For example, from the sentence "the fat cat sat on the mat," we may legitimately infer that the intrinsic intention is to present the picture of a domesticated and comfortable cat and not one of a starving alley cat. The extrinsic intention of the author can be known to us only if we have information about the extratextual context or pragmatic situation in which the text was produced. If we know, for instance, that the sentence just quoted was produced by a teacher of elementary English, we may infer that it was intended to illustrate how to pronounce the English "short *a*." If we know that the sentence was to be used in a television commercial, we may infer that it was intended to promote a particular brand of cat food. If we know that the sentence was to be used as a caption for a political cartoon, we may infer that it was intended to be satirical, with the fat cat perhaps representing the capitalist class.

Chinese poets often do provide us with information about the extratextual context in which a poem was written. However, we should not always accept their professed intentions at face value. For example, Tao Qian, in his preface to a group of poems entitled "Drinking Wine," claims that these were impromptu poems written after drinking, which he told a friend to copy down just for a laugh. Yet the poems are in fact highly serious reflections on life and his own situation, and the disclaimer of serious intent in the preface may be an attempt to forestall adverse criticism, if not political persecution, as J. R. Hightower has suggested.[57] Many other Chinese poets are fond of using the words "written in jest" in the titles of their poems, and it would be naive to take such poems literally as jests.

The four phases of understanding or interpretation interact with each other not only prospectively but also retrospectively. Our understanding of the lexical meanings of a sequence of words will place certain constraints on the possible ways in which we can construe them syntactically, yet the way we choose to construe the syntax may drastically modify our initial understanding of the lexical meaning, as the example from Su Shi quoted above demonstrates. Similarly, although it is through lexical and syntactic interpretations that we perceive the referents of words, we may initially make a mistake in identifying the referent of a word, and subsequent realization of the correct referent may force us to revise our original lexical and syntactic interpretations, as the example of Wang Wei's "Magnolia Village" shows.

Identification of the referent will in turn affect our interpretation of textual intention. As mentioned above, the name Taibai may refer to the planet Venus or a mountain or the poet Li Bai. In one of his group of fifty-nine poems, entitled "Ancient Airs" (*Gufeng*), the first line reads:

> *Taibai he cangcang*
> Taibai how gray/green/blue[58]

The word *cang*, here reduplicated for emphasis, may mean "gray," as when applied to the hair, or "green," as when applied to trees, or "blue," as when applied to the sky. Since the collective title gives no indication of the theme of each poem, it is not inconceivable, for someone reading this poem for the first time, to conjecture that the name Taibai refers to the poet himself and that the whole line means "How gray have I turned!" However, subsequent lines make it clear that the name refers to the mountain, which is described as "away from the sky by three hundred *li*" and on which a Daoist immortal is said to dwell. The poem further describes how the speaker asks the immortal for the secrets of immortality. Thus the intention of the poem is to express a wish for Daoist immortality, and since Taibai is the poet's courtesy name, we may see a pun: the poet Taibai wishes to be as enduring as the mountain Taibai.

In another of Li Bai's poems, entitled "The Barbarians Have Nobody" (*Hu wu ren*), the following line occurs:

> *Taibai ru yue di ke cui*
> Taibai enter moon enemy may destroy[59]
> [Venus enters the moon's sphere—
>      we may destroy the enemy.]

Here, Taibai clearly refers to the planet, whose supposed intrusion into the sphere of the moon the poet has taken as an omen that the enemy will be destroyed. Again, there may be a pun on the poet's own name, which implies a wish on his part to share in the military victory. Incidentally, the name Taibai here may pose a problem for translators: although referentially it is "Venus" [given the military implications], intentionally it is closer to "Mars" in connotations [for Western readers].

Determinacy in reference does not guarantee determinacy

in the interpretation of intention. On the contrary, sometimes a determinate referent may cause indeterminacy in the
interpretation of intention. Wang Wei's quatrain "Bird-Cry
Ravine" (*Niaoming jian*) opens with these lines:

> *Ren xian guihua luo*
> People at leisure cassia flowers fall
> *Ye jing chun shan kong*
> Night quiet spring mountain empty[60]

Now, the cassia is often mentioned in connection with autumn in Chinese poetry, and its appearance here may seem
to contradict the mention of spring in the next line. This
seeming contradiction can be resolved in different ways.
Some commentators assert that there is a species of cassia
that blossoms in spring or blossoms in winter and withers in
spring.[61] Alternatively, we may suggest that Wang Wei is fus-
ing two seasons and creating an imaginary world in which a
flower that normally blossoms in autumn may bloom in
spring, in the same spirit in which he reportedly painted
plantain in snow, a practice that various critics defended on
the ground that it was the inspiration of the moment that
mattered and not the physical details.[62]

Information about the extratextual context may help us interpret the textual intention. For instance, if we know that
the speaker of the sentence "I saw a man with a telescope"
was an illusionist [who includes in his act a rather bizarre
trick], we shall naturally choose the third semantic-syntactic
interpretation mentioned above. On the other hand, without
extratextual information, not only the intention but also the
semantic and syntactic interpretations may remain indeterminate, even if the referent is determinate. Unless we know
under what circumstances someone remarked, "Rose Bird is
fair," even though we know that Rose Bird is the [former]
chief justice of California, we cannot determine whether the
word "fair" means "just and impartial" or refers to the fact

that she is blonde. Thus, the four phases form a circle, which operates in both directions, forward and backward. I have described, in fact, another variation of the hermeneutic circle.

In the discussions above I have given an example from Chinese poetry as well as everyday discourse in English to suggest that questions of indeterminacy may arise in interpreting, whether intralingually or interlingually, both literary texts and quotidian speech. Of course there are differences between interpreting a literary text and interpreting someone else's speech. On the one hand, a literary text provides a verbal context for the individual words and sentences or lines, whereas an isolated sentence without any context is more indeterminate in meaning, as some of the examples given above show. On the other hand, in actual conversation we are aware of the pragmatic situation in which speech acts take place, but in reading a literary text we are often not in a position to know the original pragmatic context in which the text was written. Even when we do have extratextual information about the pragmatic context, it is debatable how far we need to take it into account in our interpretation of the text. This question brings us now to that of historicism.

As I have suggested elsewhere, *historicism* should not be confused with *historical relativism*: the former refers to the attitude that, in order to understand a text produced in another age, we must assume the mentality of a reader of that age, whereas the latter refers to the attitude that every age is bound to interpret in its own terms a text produced in another age and that no interpretation, including that of the author's own age or even of the author himself, has privileged status.[63] Traditional Chinese critics tended to favor historicism, though not of an absolute kind. This tendency can be again be traced back to Mencius, who remarked: "If we can chant [the ancients'] poetry and read their books but do not know them as people, can that be right? Therefore we discuss their age."[64]

This remark, abbreviated as "knowing the people and discussing the age [*zhi ren lun shi*]," has become a critical commonplace in Chinese. It was echoed, for instance, by Liu Xie in the chapter "The Cognoscente" (*zhiyin*, literally, "[one who] understands music," alluding to Zhong Ziqi, who alone understood the music of the zither player Boya) of *The Literary Mind*. "Now, one who composes literature [*wen*] issues forth phrases when feeling stirs, and one who reads literature opens up the text [*wen*] to penetrate into the feeling. If we follow the ripples to seek the source, even what is hidden will be revealed. The age [in which the author lived] is remote and we cannot see his face, but by observing the words [*wen*] we can immediately see his mind."[65] It will be noted that neither Mencius nor Liu Xie insists that we must become mentally the author's contemporaries in order to understand the text. All they claim is that it is possible to understand a text from an earlier age and that, to do so, it is necessary to know something about that age.

This eminently sensible attitude, with which all traditional Chinese critics would agree, seems to me compatible with Gadamer's theory of the fusion of horizons, albeit no Chinese critic ever developed a theory of historical understanding as complex and subtle as his. Here I cannot hope to give an adequate account of this theory but only quote a few key passages about the fusion of horizons from *Truth and Method*.

> In fact the horizon of the present is being continually formed, in that we have continually to test our prejudices. An important part of this testing is the encounter with the past and the understanding of the tradition from which we come. Here the horizon of the present cannot be formed without the past. There is no more an isolated horizon of the present than there are historical horizons. Understanding, rather, is always the fusion of these horizons which we imagine to exist by themselves. . . .
>
> If, however, there is no such thing as these horizons that are distinguished from one another, why do we speak of the fusion

of horizons and not simply the formation of the horizon, whose bounds are set in the depths of tradition? . . .

Historical consciousness is aware of its own otherness and hence distinguishes the horizon of tradition from its own. On the other hand, it is itself, as we are trying to show, only something laid over a continuing tradition, and hence it immediately recombines what it had distinguished in order, in the unity of the historical tradition that it thus acquires, to become again one with itself. . . .

The projecting of the historical horizon, then, is only a phase in the process of understanding, and does not become solidified into the self-alienation of a past consciousness, but is overtaken by our own present horizon of understanding. In the process of understanding there takes place a real fusion of horizons, which means that as the historical horizon is projected, it is simultaneously removed.[66]

Gadamer's theory involves a paradox: through consciousness of one's own historicity, one can transcend one's present horizon and achieve a fusion of horizons. According to David Couzzens Hoy, "In fact, Gadamer's position can be seen as trying to go beyond Nietzsche precisely by turning paradox into paradigm. In Gadamer's theory this hermeneutical consciousness of the need for historical self-understanding is not only an essential condition for understanding, but also paradigmatic for it."[67] Although Gadamer does not deal specifically with interlingual and transcultural interpretation, his theory should be applicable, *mutatis mutandis*, to the fusion of cultural horizons. This inference is implicit in his statement, "Just as the individual is never simply an individual, because he is always involved with others, so too the closed horizon that is supposed to enclose a culture is an abstraction."[68] The fusion of cultural horizons, then, is both possible and necessary. Paradoxically, by becoming aware of the unspoken presuppositions as well as consciously held beliefs of one culture, a person may hope to transcend them and understand those of another culture.

I have been trying to encourage such awareness in the preceding pages. But perhaps interpretation is ultimately bound to move perpetually between the impossibility of perfect understanding and the necessity for imperfect explication, just as poetry is bound to move perpetually between the voice of silence and the silence of the void.

# Afterword: Impersonal Personality

I wish to challenge here a common assumption that lyric poetry is personal in nature. In dealing with Chinese poetry, we are immediately confronted with the problems of terminology. The word "lyric" is usually translated into Chinese as *shuqing shi*, which literally means "poetry expressing emotion." This rendering seems to give the term too narrow a definition, excluding from it such other kinds of nonnarrative and nondramatic poetry as those expressing philosophical views or reflections on history or social criticism. Perhaps we might substitute the term *biaoxian shi* ("expressive poetry"), which does not specify *what* is being expressed, in contradistinction to *xushi shi* ("narrative poetry") and *xiju shi* ("dramatic poetry"). The problem, however, is more complicated. Several genres of Chinese poetry all have some claim to being called "lyric," yet none of them is exclusively nonnarrative and nondramatic. Apart from the generically ambiguous *fu*,[1] all major Chinese poetic genres were originally sung and hence may be considered lyric in the original sense of a poem sung to the accompaniment of a lyre.

Even if we disregard etymology and define lyric simply as "nonnarrative and nondramatic poetry," the problem is still with us. The *shi*, the oldest and most venerable of all Chinese poetic genres, is generally short and nonnarrative, but it includes also some fairly long narrative poems, not to mention dramatic monologues and dialogues. The *yuefu* ("music department songs") include many narrative ballads as well as love songs.[2] The *ci* ("lyric meters") [flourished from the late ninth through the thirteenth centuries, with a renaissance during the Qing era] involves hundreds of intricate metrical patterns based on musical tunes and generally expresses personal emotion or thought, but some works in this genre contain elaborate description or narration, and others are dramatic monologues or dialogues. The *qu* ("lyric songs," or "dramatic lyrics") [flourished in the thirteenth and fourteenth centuries (the Jin and Yuan eras), with further developments throughout the remainder of the traditional period], which also involves hundreds of metrical patterns based on a different, later repertoire of musical tunes, may be incorporated in full-length drama or exist independently as *sanqu* ("scattered songs"), including single songs known as *xiaoling* ("little airs") and song suites known as *taoshu* ("suite numbers") or *santao* ("scattered suites"). However, even in the case of *sanqu*, a song or suite may form a dramatic monologue and may be satirical or comic rather than expressing the author's personal emotions. Thus, to subsume all these Chinese poetic genres under the rubric "lyric" would not be helpful, for distinctions between any two genres would no longer be observable; nor are we justified in identifying any single genre exclusively with the "lyric."

I intend here not to solve this problem but simply to call attention to its existence. Meanwhile, I shall continue to use the term "lyric" to mean nonnarrative and nondramatic poetry in discussing whether all lyric poetry is personal in character.

We may begin by looking at two extremely well-known Chinese poems that appear to be impersonal. I shall present here the bare semantic-syntactic bones of these poems.

### Deer Enclosure

[On] empty mountains, not seeing people;
Only hear people's talk echo.
Reflected sunlight enters deep woods,
Again shines upon the green moss.

—WANG WEI (701–761)[3]

### River Snow

[From] a thousand mountains, birds' flight ceases.
[On] a myriad paths, people's footprints vanish.
[In] a solitary boat, a rain-cloaked,
    straw-hatted old man
Alone fishes the cold river's snow.

—LIU ZONGYUAN (773–819)[4]

Most people will perhaps agree that these are lyric poems: they are certainly neither narrative nor dramatic. Yet they do not express any personal emotions but may be considered illustrations of what the critic Wang Guowei calls "the world without an 'I' [*wu wo zhi jing*]," of which more will be said later. Nevertheless, these poems are not "impersonal" in a cold, objective sense, for each presents a personal vision of the world (or rather a created world) that is rooted in, but not identical with, the poet's own lived world (*Lebenswelt*).[5]

We may now compare these two poems with two well-known examples of English poetry.

### Song

A widow bird sate mourning her love,
    Upon a winter bough.
The frozen wind crept on above,
    The freezing stream below.
There was no leaf upon the forest bare,
    No flowers upon the ground,
And little motion in the air
    Except the mill-wheel's sound.

—P. B. SHELLEY (1792–1822)[6]

*From "Little Gidding"*

Midwinter spring is its own season
Sempiternal though sodden towards sundown,
Suspended in time, between pole and tropic,
When the short day is brightest, with frost and fire,
The brief sun flames the ice on pond and ditches,
In windless cold that is the heart's heat,
Reflecting in a watery mirror
A glare that is blindness in the early afternoon.

—T. S. ELIOT (1888–1965)[7]

Although Shelley's poem may have been intended to be used in the unfinished drama *Charles the First*, it can certainly stand on its own as a lyric. It was published simply as "A Song" in the *Posthumous Poems*, and it was not connected with the drama until W. M. Rossetti's edition of Shelley's poems.[8] Eliot's lines, are admittedly from a longish poem, which in turn forms part of a still longer work, *Four Quartets*, yet they can serve to illustrate certain comparable points among all the four works quoted.

In none of the poems does the personality of the poet intrude upon the scene. The phrase "the heart's heat" (not "*my* heart's heat") in Eliot's lines need not be taken as a reference to the author but should rather be taken as an impersonal reference to any one with a heart. Certain images and motifs occur in two or more of the poems: sunset, winter, solitude, and the absence or near-absence of people and of action. Of course, their significance varies from poem to poem. Wang Wei, with his tendency to see things in Buddhist terms, views the phenomenal world as illusory: the mountain is empty (*kong*, which is also the Chinese translation of the Sanskrit *śūnyatā*); the reflected light of the setting sun and the echoes of human speech add to the impression of insubstantiality and also suggest the limitations of human perception, as Pauline Yu has observed.[9] Liu Zongyuan's poem has been interpreted in purely Chan terms by Du Songbo,[10] but since, as I remarked earlier, Chan is a synthesis of Buddhism and philosophical Daoism, it is not always possible to distinguish Chan and Daoism. I propose to interpret the poem in a Daoist perspective. The tiny figure of the solitary fisherman against the vast background of mountains, rivers, and infinite space implies the insignificance of human beings when compared with nature. Furthermore, the fisherman is a conventional Daoist symbol of withdrawal from society and return to nature, and his seemingly futile efforts to fish in the cold river suggests his indifference to success or failure. To a Daoist, life and death, spring and winter, and day and night are all relative rather than opposite states of being, and the seemingly bleak landscape betokens not sadness but only detachment.

In contrast, Shelley's poem is permeated with sadness. Here, winter is identified with death, as indicated by the first line and reinforced by the first two lines of the second stanza. Yet Shelley had written elsewhere, "If Winter comes, can spring be far behind?" Perhaps the self-avowed atheist could not bear to adopt a totally pessimistic view of life. In Eliot's lines, as may be expected from a devout Christian, the turning point from winter to spring suggests resurrection and redemption, and the opposition between heat and cold is reconciled, though in a manner different from that of the Daoist. In spite of the differences in philosophical orientations, each of these poems captures a moment in time and renders it timeless, thus turning personal vision into impersonal truth.

We turn now from poetry to poetics. Although traditional Chinese poetics was dominated to a large extent by the expressive theory of poetry epitomized in the saying *shi yan zhi* ("poetry verbalizes intent"), attributed to the sage-emperor Shun (traditional dates 2255–2208 B.C.) and therefore sacrosanct, many Chinese poets and critics in fact emphasized the impersonal, which is often identified with the cosmic Dao, or at least advocated a fusion of *qing* ("feeling," or "inner experience") and *jing* ("scene," or "external environment"), or of *wu* ("object," or "thing") and *wo* ("subject," or "I"). The critics discussed in this volume all sought something transcending the personal, whether they called it "meaning beyond words," "inspired mood," "ineffable flavor," or "spirit and tone."

Mention has already been made of Wang Guowei's concept of "the world without an 'I' " in poetry. Let us now look at this more closely in the context in which the phrase occurs. "There is a world with an 'I' and there is a world without an 'I.' . . . In the world with an 'I,' it is I who look at objects, and therefore everything is tinged with my color. In the world without an 'I,' it is one object that looks at other objects, and therefore one no longer knows which is 'I' and which is 'object.' "[11] In other words, in the former world the poets look at external objects through their subjective emotions, whereas in the latter world they identify with the objects they are contemplating. In the former case, their personality is obviously present in their poems, while in the latter case there is no sign of their personality, yet the poems cannot be called totally impersonal, since they embody a personal vision. The world without an "I" should be understood as self-transcendence, not self-extinction, for if the self has really become extinct, then who is writing the poem?

In the West, the mimetic concept of poetry, based largely on epic and drama, dominated poetics from Aristotle to the Romantic Movement. The romanticists, of course, emphasized self-expression, but some of them also strove for impersonal personality. Keats's familiar remarks about identifying with a sparrow and about the poet's being "the most unpoetic of any thing in existence, because he has no Identity"[12] are remarkably similar to Su Shi's lines about a painter's identification with the bamboos he painted.

> When Yuke [Wen Tong, 1019–1079] painted bamboos,
> He saw only bamboos but no man;
> Not only did he see no man,

> But he had left his dissolved body,
> His body transformed with the bamboos,
> Producing endless limpidity and freshness.[13]

Furthermore, Keats's concept of "negative capability," which is the capability of "being in uncertainties, Mysteries, doubts, without any irritable reaching after fact and reason,"[14] may be considered another dimension of impersonal personality and reminds one of Yan Yu's remark that "poetry involves a separate kind of meaning [or interest], which is not concerned with reason."

Some symbolists who reacted against romanticism aimed at impersonality. For instance, Mallarmé wrote to his friend Henri Cazalis, "I am now impersonal and no longer the Stéphane you knew—but an aptitude of the spiritual universe for seeing and developing itself through what I was."[15] This concept of the poet as the vehicle through which the spiritual universe finds its voice is clearly similar to the Chinese concept of the poet as the vehicle through which the Dao finds its voice.

Among postsymbolist poets, Eliot perhaps provides the best illustration of the paradox of impersonal personality. On the one hand, he asserted: "Poetry is not a turning loose of emotion, but an escape from emotion; it is not an expression of personality, but an escape from personality. But, of course, only those who have personality and emotions know what it means to want to escape from these things."[16] On the other hand, he also remarked, "A man may, hypothetically, compose a number of fine passages or even whole poems which could each give satisfaction, and yet not be a great poet, unless we felt them to be united by one significant, consistent and developing personality."[17]

Like most Chinese critics, Eliot does not always use his key critical terms in the same sense but uses them in various senses, some of which may seem contradictory to each other, in different contexts. As Fei-pai Lu has ably demonstrated,

Eliot's seeming self-contradictions are really parts of the dialectical structure of his theory of poetry, and the terms "impersonality" and "personality" can have both positive and negative meanings. According to Lu:

> The term impersonality is subject to a dialectical doubling: one good and one bad. In its good sense, impersonality refers to the universal in the particular, the absolute in its plurality. Good "impersonality" is found in the poet who, out of intense personal experience, is able to express a general truth; retaining all the particularity of the experience, to make it a general symbol. In its bad sense, impersonality refers to generality not sanctioned by particular experience.[18]

Or, in the words of Mowbray Allan, "In *The Sacred Wood* it is implied that there is a false impersonality which results from the uncritical acceptance of the values and opinions of society and that a strong personality is necessary to 'slough off' this false impersonality and achieve a true impersonality: submission of the individual will to the laws of the universe."[19] Likewise, the term "personality" may be used in a good or a bad sense. In the good sense, it means the poet's "particular comprehension of life" or "point of view"; in a bad sense, it means an inability to transcend one's self, whereas the personal point of view advocated by Eliot is not solipsistic, as Mowbray Allan points out.

Despite philosophical differences between Eliot and Chinese critics, his concept of "point of view" as "the emotional equivalent of ideas" is comparable to such Chinese concepts as *wei* ("flavor"), *yun* ("tone"), *xingqu* ("inspired mood"), and *jingjie* ("world"), espoused by various critics, some of whom have been discussed in the preceding pages. Furthermore, like some Chinese critics, Eliot also believed in the inseparability of subject and object, He wrote: "Consciousness, we shall find, is reducible to relations between objects, and objects we shall find to be reducible to relations between different states of consciousness; and neither point of view is more nearly ultimate than the other. But if we attempt to put the world together again, after having divided it into consciousness and objects, we are condemned to failure."[20]

So far we have been concerned with impersonal personality chiefly at the philosophical level, with reference to the poet's interaction with the world. We may now turn our attention to the artistic level, with reference to the poet's creative process. At this level, the relationship between personality and impersonality may be formulated in various ways. In Chinese, this relationship may be discussed in terms of *cai* ("talent") versus *xue* ("learning"), or *xingling* ("native sensibility") versus *gelü* ("norms and rules"), or *bian* ("change") versus *zheng* ("orthodoxy"), or *chuangxin* ("original innovation") versus *yanxi* ("following tradition").[21] In English, the relationship may be discussed in terms of "nature" versus "art," or "individual talent" versus "tradition," or "originality" versus "imitation," or "romanticism" versus "classicism."

Some Chinese critics emphasized personality, intuition, inspiration, talent, spontaneity, and innovation, while others stressed learning, convention, tradition, technique, and imitation of ancient poets. The most discerning critics tended to strike a balance between the two sets of desiderata, or see them in a paradoxical relationship. For instance, Liu Xie laid equal emphasis on *xingqing* ("personal nature") and *taoran* ("molding and dyeing," i.e. cultivation). "Talent may be ordinary or outstanding, the vital force may be strong or gentle, learning may be superficial or profound, practice may be refined or vulgar: these are all what one's personal nature has smelted or what gradual cultivation has crystallized."[22] Also, as we have seen, Yan Yu advocated intuition on the one hand and learning on the other, a seeming contradiction that can be resolved.

A later critic, Ye Xie (1627–1703), wrote:

One who writes poetry must see where the ancients placed mandates on themselves, where they focused their eyes, where they set their goals, where they commanded their words, where they started with their hands—none of which may be treated casually. He must thoroughly remove his own original visage, as a physician treats a chronic disease: first completely purging the accumulated filth to put the pure emptiness in order, then gradually filling it with the learning, judgment, spirit, and reason of the ancients. After a long time, he must be able to remove the visage of the ancients; only then can the mind of a master craftsman emerge.[23]

In other words, one must first get rid of one's own personality, then assume the personality of an ancient poet, and finally discard this second personality and achieve an impersonal personality.

If Eliot were aware of such Chinese texts as these, he might well have concurred with Ye Xie on various points. Both of them recognized the importance of tradition as well as individual talent, and both believed that tradition required not only continuity but also change. Naturally, there are differences of opinion and emphasis between the two. Ye Xie, writing against the archaists who advocated imitation of ancient poets of particular periods, placed special emphasis on individual talent, courage, judgment, and strength, whereas Eliot, writing against the postromantic emphasis on originality, declared that in poetry there is no absolute originality that owes nothing to the past and that "the most individual parts of [a poet's] works may be those in which the dead poets, his ancestors, assert their immortality most rigorously."[24] Furthermore, Ye and Eliot conceived of poetic history in somewhat similar terms. Ye saw the history of Chinese poetry after the Song period as an endless series of alternations between flowering and withering,[25] while Eliot saw the history of European poetry as an endless series of readjustments of the existing order. In both cases, individual

talent is needed to bring about the reflorescence or readjust-
ment, but the mainstream of poetry, which is impersonal, remains basically the same. Eliot's own poetry illustrates beau-
tifully the interaction between tradition and individual talent.
The lines from "Little Gidding" quoted above, as Helen
Gardner pointed out, owe something to Langland for their
rhythmic structure, but Eliot has avoided Langland's monot-
ony and given the lines much greater freedom.[26]

The paradox of impersonal personality can also be discussed at the hermeneutic level, with reference to the reading process. Here, personality may be identified with either
the author or the reader, and the impersonality with the text.
The relationship between personality and impersonality can
also be formulated in terms of the reader's interaction with a
hermeneutic tradition. This aspect of impersonal personality
has been discussed above in chapter 4.

# Chinese Words
and Names

Bai, Duke of 白公
*baima fei ma* 白馬非馬
Baoxi 庖犧
*bi yi yi shifei ci yi yi shifei* 彼亦一是非此亦一是非
*bian* 變 (change)
*bian* 辨 (discrimination)
*bian* 辯 (eloquence)
*biaoxian shi* 表現詩
*can* 參
*can* Chan 參禪
*can shi* 參詩
Cang Jie 倉頡
Cao Cao 曹操
Cao Pi 曹丕
Cao Zhi 曹植
Chan 禪
*Changgeng* 長更
Chen Yi 陳鎰
Chen Zi'ang 陳子昂
*chenzhuo tongkuai* 沈着痛快
Chu 楚
*chuangxin* 創新
*chuanxin* 傳心

*chugai* 除改

*chuzhuo* 觸着

*ci* 詞

*congrong bupo* 從容不迫

Cui Hao 崔顥

Dahui 大慧

Dai Fugu 戴復古

Dai Kui 戴逵

*Daojia* 道家

*Daojiao* 道教

*dizhi* 地支

*Du shi xue yin* 杜詩學引

*fan'an* 翻案

Fang Wen 方文

*fu* 賦

Fuxi 伏羲

*gelü* 格律

Gao Ke 高苛

*gaomiao* 高妙

*Gaotang fu* 高唐賦

*gong'an* 公案

Gongsun Chou 公孫丑

Gongsun Long 公孫龍

Guanxiu 貫休

Guo Xiang 郭象

Han Yu 韓愈

*hanxu* 含蓄

He Ning 和凝

He Youwen 何友聞

*hongxing zhitou chunyi nao Shangshu* 紅杏枝頭春意鬧尙書

Hou Ying 侯贏

*Huajian ji* 花間集

*huajing* 化境

Huang Di 黃帝

Huang Tingjian 黃庭堅

*huiyi* 會意

Jian, Prince 太子建

Jiangxi School 江西派

*jie* 解 (understand/interpret)

*jie* 偈 (Buddhist chant/hymn)

Jing Ke 荊軻

*Jing xi zi zhi* 敬惜字紙

*jingjie* 境界

*Jingnu* 靜女

*Jinxing* 金星

*Jiubian* 九辨

*keyi yi hui bukeyi yan chuan* 可以意會不可以言傳

*kong* 空

Lao Dan 老聃

Lao Zi 老子

*li* 理

Li Erh 李耳

Li Houzhu 李後主

Li Liweng 李笠翁

Li Quyan 李去言

Li Shan 李善

Li Yu 李煜

Li Yue 李約

Li Zhiyi 李之儀

Lie Yukou 列御寇

*lingyin* 令尹

Lisao 離騷

Liu Zongyuan 柳宗元

*liushu* 六書

Luo Binwang 羅賓王

Mei Yaochen 梅堯臣

Meicun 梅村

Mengchang, Prince of 孟嘗君

*miaowu* 妙悟

*ming* 名

*mingjia* 名家

*mingyue songjian zhao* 明月松間照

*nao* 鬧

Niaoming *jian* 鳥鳴澗

*nong* 弄

*nü* 女

Pei Di 裴迪

*peng* 鵬

*pianwen* 駢文

Ping, King of Chu 楚平王

*Pipa xing* 琵琶行

Qi 齊

*qi* 氣

*qiang* 强

*qiao duo tiangong* 巧多天工

Qiming 啓明

*qin* 琴

*qing* 情

*qingkong* 清空

*qu* 趣 (mood, interest, etc.)

*qu* 曲 (song)

Qu Yuan 屈原

*quan* 荃(筌) (bait/trap)

*quzi ci* 曲子詞

Ren An 任安

*ren chang wu yan er wu bu yan* 人常無言而無不言

*renzhe jian ren zhizhe jian zhi* 仁者見仁智者見智

*ru* 汝

Ruan Ji 阮籍

*sanqu* 散曲

*santao* 散套

Sengzhao 僧肇

*shan* 山

*shanhu* 珊瑚

*shen* 神

Shen Quanqi 沈佺期

*shensi* 神思

*shenyun* 神韻

*shi* 詩 (poetry)

*shi* 勢 (sweep)

*shi wu da gu* 詩無達詁

*shi yan zhi* 詩言志

*Shige* 詩格

*Shouwei yin* 首尾吟

*shu bujin yan yan bujin yi* 書不盡言言不盡意

*shu buneng jinyan* 書不能盡言

*si wu xie* 思無邪

Sima Qian 司馬遷

*sizhi* 思致

Song Jingwen 宋景文

Song Qi 宋祁

Song Yu 宋玉

Song Zhiwen 宋之問

*sudi* 俗諦

Taibai 太白

*taizai* 太宰

*taoran* 陶染

*taoshu* 套數

*tiangan* 天干

*tuori dai ke wei qu jin qi miao* 他日殆可謂曲盡其妙

Wang Anshi 王安石

Wang Huizhi 王徽之

Wang Shizhen 王世貞 (1526–1590)

Wang Shizhen 王士禎 (1634–1711)

Wang Yuanmei 王元美

*wei* 味

*Weishu* 魏書

*wen* 文

Wen, Emperor of Wei 魏文帝

Wen Tong 文同

Wenbo Xuezi 溫伯雪子

*wu* 無 (absence)

*wu* 物 (thing)

Wu, Emperor of Wei 魏武帝

Wu Mengchuang 吳夢窗

Wu Weiye 吳偉業

Wu Wenying 吳文英

*wu wo zhih jing* 無我之境

*wu yan yan* 無言言

Wu Zhi 吳質

*wujing* 悟境

*Wuliu Xiansheng zhuan* 五柳先生傳

*wuqian yan* 五千言

*Wuxi ji xu* 午溪集序

*wuxing* 五行

*xian* 仙

*xiang* 象

Xiangjun 湘君

*xiaoling* 小令

*Xici zhuan* 繫辭傳

Xie Lingyun 謝靈運

Xie Zhou 謝晝

*xiju shi* 戲劇詩

*xinghui* 興會

*xingling* 性靈

*xingqing* 性情

*xingqu* 興趣

*xingrong* 形容

Xinyi *wu* 辛夷塢

*xishuai* 蟋蟀

Xu Rui 徐瑞

*xue* 學

*xushi shi* 叙事詩

Xuzhi 序志

*yan* 言

Yan Shu 晏殊

Yan Wei 嚴維

*yan wu yan* 言無言

Yang Jiong 楊炯

Yang Wanli 楊萬里

*yanxi* 沿襲

Yaofu 堯夫

*ye* 也 (exclamatory particle)

*ye* 邪 (interrogative particle)

*yi* 意

*yi guo yu yan* 意過于言

*Yi Jing* 易經

*yi qi you ji yi you suo ji* 議其有極議有所極

*yingwu* 鸚鵡

*Yinjiu* 飲酒

*Yinxiu* 隱秀

*yiqu* 意趣

*yixiang* 意象

*you* 有

*yuefu* 樂府

*yun* 韻

*yunpo yuelai hua nong ying Langzhong* 雲破月來花弄影郎中

*zai* 宰

*zaixiang* 宰相
Zeng Gong 曾鞏
Zeng Ji 曾幾
Zhang Sanying 張三影
Zhang Xian 張先
Zhao Wen 昭文
Zhaoming, Prince 昭明太子
*zhendi* 眞諦
*zheng* 正
Zheng 鄭
Zheng Banqiao 鄭板橋
Zheng Xie 鄭燮
*zhengming* 正名
*zhi* 志
*zhi ren lun shi* 知人論世
*zhiyin* 知音
Zhuang Zhou 莊周
Zigong 子貢
Zilu 子路
Zuozhuan 左傳

# Abbreviations

| | |
|---|---|
| *CLEAR* | *Chinese Literature: Essays, Articles, Reviews* |
| *CLS* | *Comparative Literature Studies* |
| *CSJC* | *Congshu jicheng* 叢書集成 |
| *GDWL* | *Gudai wenxuelilun yanjiu* 古代文學理論研究 |
| *GXJB* | *Guoxue jiben congshu* 國學基本叢書 |
| *HJAS* | *Harvard Journal of Asiatic Studies* |
| *HYSI* | *Harvard-Yenching Institute Sinological Index Series* |
| *JCP* | *Journal of Chinese Philosophy* |
| *QTS* | *Quan Tang shi* 全唐詩 |
| *SBBY* | *Sibu beiyao* 四部備要 |
| *SBCK* | *Sibu congkan* 四部叢刊 |
| *SKZM* | *Siku quanshu zongmu* 四庫全書總目 |
| *TR* | *Tamkang Review* |
| *WJNB* | *Wei Jin Nanbeichao wenxue shi cankao ziliao* 魏晉南北朝文學史參考資料 |
| *ZGWP* | *Zhongguo wenxuepiping ziliao huibian* 中國文學批評資料彙編 |

# Notes

*Introduction*

1. Lindenberger 1984, p. 18.
2. Miner 1983, p. 70.

*Chapter 1. The Paradox of Language*

1. Brooks 1947, pp. 3–20.
2. [This incident is the supposed origin of Chan (Zen) Buddhism, the truth of which lies beyond words. Gautama Śākyamuni (sixth century B.C.) is the historical Buddha.] This legend has been told in Chinese innumerable times. For an English version, see Wu 1967, p. 30.
3. Derrida 1976, p. 99.
4. Gao Heng 1956, p. 1.
5. Qian Zhongshu 1979, vol. 2, pp. 403–406. The title, literally "Pipe-Awl Collection," alludes to the *Zhuang Zi*, chapter 17: "This is just like using a pipe to peep at the sky or an awl to point at the earth."
6. Hansen 1983, p. 67.
7. Ibid., p. 71.
8. Lau 1963, p. 57. His 1982 version (pp. 266–267), based on the Mawangdui manuscript copies discovered in 1973, is not basically different. For some other translations, see Creel 1983.
9. Hansen 1983, p. 67.

10. For a different arrangement of the parts, based on the Mawangdui texts, see *Lao Zi zhushi*.

11. I have added the word *qiang* to the second half of the sentence, following Li Yue. See Yan Lingfeng 1954, pp. 8–9.

12. See Derrida 1976, pp. xiv–xviii. [In other words, ultimate reality as something "signified" admits of no pure "signifier," and any name for it *must* be provisional. Derrida, in fact, is even more radical, for he denies the possibility of "pure" signification for anything signified; see Magliola 1984, pp. 16–18.]

13. Gao Heng 1956, p. 119. Cf. Lau 1963, p. 117.

14. Quoted in Hofstadter 1979, p. 17.

15. Bai Juyi, *houji, juan* 13, 1a; see also Liu 1982b.

16. Qian Zhongshu 1979, vol. 2, pp. 413, 456–458.

17. Gao Heng 1956, p. 100. Cf. Lau 1963, p. 106.

18. Gao Heng 1956, p. 148.

19. Ibid.

20. E.g. Lau 1963, p. 140.

21. Gao Heng 1956, p. 152. Cf. Lau, 1963, p. 143.

22. For the text, see Wang Liqi [1952] 1968, p. 88. The translation has previously appeared in Liu 1975, p. 51. Cf. Shih 1959, p. 175.

23. Graham 1981, p. 56.

24. For the text, see *Zhuang Zi yinde*, 5/2/53. The translation has already appeared in Liu 1975, p. 62. Cf. Watson 1968, p. 43; Graham 1981, p. 56.

25. *Zhuang Zi yinde*, 5/2/55. Cf. Watson 1968, p. 43; Graham 1981, p. 57.

26. *Zhuang Zi yinde*, 5/2/59. Cf. Watson 1968, p. 43.

27. Graham 1981, p. 57.

28. In translating the word *dao* as "speech," I am following Cheng Xuanying, as quoted in Guo Qingfan [1894] 1961, p. 489.

29. The translation of this sentence is also based on Cheng Xuanying.

30. *Zhuang Zi yinde*, 36/13/64. Cf. Watson 1968, p. 152; Graham 1981, p. 139.

31. *Zhuang Zi yinde*, 36/13/70. The translation has appeared in Liu 1979, p. 45. Cf. Watson 1968, p. 152; Graham 1981, p. 139.

32. *Zhuang Zi yinde*, 67/24/66. Cf. Watson 1968, p. 271.

33. *Zhuang Zi yinde*, 73/25/80. The translation is based on Guo

Xiang (d. A.D. 312), as quoted in Guo Qingfan [1894] 1961, p. 919. Cf. Watson 1968, p. 293; Graham 1981, p. 153.

34. Magliola 1984, p. 19. For other similarities between Zhuang Zi and Derrida, see Yeh 1983.

35. *Zhuang Zi yinde*, 75/26/48. Some commentators take *quan* as "bait" instead of "trap." Cf. Watson 1968, p. 302; Graham 1981, p. 190; Wu 1982, p. 55; Zhang 1985, p. 394.

36. *Zhuang Zi yinde*, 4/22/23.

37. Ma Qichang [1894] 1953, *juan* 1, 9b. For other translations, see Watson 1968, p. 39; Graham 1981, p. 52.

38. *Zhuang Zi yinde*, 7/25/35. Cf. Watson 1968, p. 285; Graham 1981, p. 109.

39. *Zhuang Zi yinde*, 73/25/81. For the last sentence I am adopting the reading *yi qi you ji* instead of *yi you suo ji*. See Guo Qingfan [1894] 1961, p. 919. Cf. Watson 1968, p. 293; Graham 1981, p. 153.

40. *Zhuang Zi yinde*, 75/27/6. Cf. Graham 1981, p. 153.

41. Ma Qichang [1894] 1953, *juan* 7, 7b.

42. Watson 1968, p. 304.

43. Gao Heng 1956, p. 82.

44. Magliola 1984, p. 91.

45. Ibid., pp. 105, 210 n.83.

46. See Wu 1982, pp. 11, 4.

47. Yang Bojun 1958, pp. 220–243.

48. Ibid., pp. 159–160. Cf. Graham 1960, pp. 166–167.

49. Plato, *Phaedrus*, quoted in Wimsatt and Brooks 1965, p. 64; *Republic*, quoted in ibid., pp. 10–11.

50. Plato 1925, pp. 96–97; quoted in Qian Zhongshu 1979, vol. 2, p. 410.

51. Liu [1962] 1983, pp. 3–6.

52. Peirce 1932, pp. 143, 159–165.

53. Karlgren 1972, p. 115. "Archaic Chinese" is Karlgren's term for the language of the early Zhou era (ca. 1100–600 B.C.). Some other scholars call this language Old Chinese.

54. Peirce 1932, pp. 159–165.

55. Karlgren 1972, p. 112.

56. Ibid., p. 191.

57. Ibid., p. 273.

58. Ibid., p. 49.

59. Peirce 1932, p. 69; quoted in Derrida 1976, p. 48.
60. Saussure 1974; quoted in Derrida 1976, p. 48.
61. See Liu 1975, pp. 18, 23, 25.
62. Duan Yucai, *juan* 15, p. 1.
63. See Liu 1975, pp. 22–24.
64. See Liu [1962] 1983, p. 6.
65. Ibid., pp. 3–7.
66. Derrida 1967, p. 92.
67. Kenner 1975–1976, pp. 89–97.
68. Liu 1982a, p. 42.
69. Kenner 1975–1976, p. 93.
70. Gao Heng 1956, p. 26. Cf. Lau 1963, p. 67.
71. See Derrida 1976, p. lxv.
72. Gao Heng 1956, pp. 16–18. Cf. Lau 1963, p. 62.
73. Wesling 1980, p. 95.
74. Ibid., pp. 110–111.
75. Magliola 1984, p. 91.
76. Zhang 1985, pp. 391–392, 394–395.
77. Magliola 1984, pp. 90–91, quoting Chang 1975, pp. 74–75. For the interpolation, see Lau 1963, p. 85.
78. See Liu 1975, pp. 21–25, 121–122.
79. Zhang 1985, p. 397.
80. *Lunyu yinde*, 36/17/17.
81. Ibid., 30/14/38.
82. Sun Xingyan, p. 604.
83. Zhang 1985, p. 394.
84. Hansen 1983, p. 98.
85. Wang Zhongling 1983, p. 78.
86. This sentence is quoted in the biography of Sima Qian in Ban Gu [A.D. 32–92], *juan* 62. For J. R. Hightower's translation of this letter, see Birch 1965, pp. 95–102.
87. Merleau-Ponty 1962, p. 389.
88. *Meng Zi yinde*, 11/2a/6. Cf. Lau 1970, p. 77.
89. *Meng Zi yinde*, 24/3b/9. Cf. Lau 1970, p. 115.
90. *Xun Zi yinde*, 83/17/25. Cf. Hansen 1983, pp. 79–81; Watson 1963, pp. 139–156. [Burton Watson translates *ming wu gu yi* as "names have no intrinsic appropriateness." Cf. Watson 1963, p. 144.]
91. See Kao and Obenchain 1975, pp. 285–324.

92. Yang Xiong, *juan* 4, p. 14. For more information on Yang, see Knechtges 1981. For a German translation of Yang's *Fa yan*, see Zach 1939.
93. Yang Xiong, *juan* 4, p. 14.
94. Ibid., *juan* 6, p. 24.
95. The term *fan an* refers to legal cases and means "reversing the verdict." Applied to literature, it means "deliberately reversing previous opinions."
96. Ouyang Jian in Ouyang Xun 1965, *juan* 19, and Yan Kejun [1815] 1959, *Quan Jin wen, juan* 109; text quoted in *ZGWP*, vol. 1, p. 204.
97. Cf. Qian Zhongshu 1979, vol. 4, p. 1219. For other interpretations and criticisms of Ouyang Jian's essay, see Yuan Xingpei 1979, pp. 129–130, and Wang Zhongling 1983, pp. 88–90.
98. See Ch'ien 1984, p. 386.
99. Huijiao, *juan* 8, p. 30a.
100. Ibid.
101. See Wu 1967, p. 75.
102. See Cleary and Cleary 1977.
103. Zhou Chi, preface to *Biyan lu*, p. 3.
104. Liu Yan, in *ZGWP*, vol. 3, p. 341.
105. For Confucian pragmatic views of literature, see Liu 1975, pp. 106–116.
106. Yuan Zongdao 1935, p. 253. The translation has appeared in Liu 1975, p. 80.
107. For the archaists, see Liu 1975, pp. 36–37, 90–92; for a comparison of the archaists and anti-archaists such as Yuan, see Lynn 1983a.

*Chapter 2. The Metaparadox of Poetics*

1. The *fu* is a mixed genre of prose and poetry, known in English variously as "poetic essay," "prose poem," "rhymeprose," "exposition," and "rhapsody," none of which is the exact equivalent of *fu*.
2. Lu Ji in *WJNB*, pp. 253–254. Cf. the versions of Ch'en Shih-hsiang (1965, p. 240) and of Achilles Fang ([1951] 1965, pp. 6–7).
3. Qian Zhongshu 1979, vol. 3, pp. 1180–1181.

4. Cf. Karlgren 1974, p. 102. Most commentators take "this young person" to refer to the bride, but Gao Heng (1980, p. 213) understands it to refer to the matchmaker.

5. This passage was translated previously in Liu 1975, p. 73.

6. See Hightower 1968, pp. 2–44.

7. Tao Qian, *juan* 3, 17a; cf. Hightower 1968, p. 14; Davis 1983, vol. 1, p. 96.

8. See note 26 to chapter 1.

9. Liu 1975, p. 125.

10. Wang Liqi [1952] 1968, p. 81; cf. Shih 1959, p. 156.

11. Wang Yuanhua 1979, p. 111.

12. Zhou Zhenfu 1981, p. 299.

13. Liu 1975, pp. 21–25, 33–34, 74–77, 122–126.

14. Wang Liqi [1952] 1968, p. 81; cf. Shih 1959, pp. 157–158.

15. The pitcher is an allusion to the *Zuo zhuan*, seventh year of Duke Zhao (534 B.C.). For the pipe, see note 5 to chapter 1.

16. Wang Liqi [1952] 1968, p. 130; cf. Shih 1959, pp. 7–8.

17. Liu 1975, pp. 75, 128–129.

18. Shao Yong, 1066, *juan* 20, 2a; quoted in *ZGWP*, vol. 3, p. 151.

19. See note 89 to chapter 1.

20. Lu Ji, 1961, p. 270. The editors of *WJNB* are mistaken in saying that Lu thought the "supreme broth" tasteless; what he did say is that some writings lacked even the bland but lingering taste of the "supreme broth."

21. Shen Yue, quoted in Tao Qian, biographical section, 3b; cf. Davis 1983, vol. 2, pp. 173, 185.

22. See Liu 1975, pp. 128–129.

23. Fokkema 1978, pp. 162–163.

24. Li He 1958, p. 154. A slightly different translation has appeared in Liu 1982a, p. 9.

25. Qian Zhongshu [1948] 1965, pp. 71–73.

26. *Lunyu yinde*, 36/17/16.

27. Jiang Kui, p. 5a. Cf. Lin 1983, p. 297.

28. Wittgenstein 1961, p. 151.

29. He Jingming [1531] 1555, *juan* 32, 20a; quoted in *ZGWP*, vol. 8, p. 319.

30. Li Mengyang [1531] 1602, *juan* 62, 7b; quoted in *ZGWP*, vol. 8, p. 292.

31. Quoted in Guo Shaoyu 1956, p. 302. A slightly different translation appeared in Liu [1962] 1983, p. 79.

32. Li Mengyang [1531] 1602, *juan* 62, 13a–13b; quoted in *ZGWP*, vol. 8, p. 295. The translation has appeared in Liu [1962] 1983, p. 80.

33. Pope 1962, p. 6.

34. Ibid., p. 7.

35. Qian Qianyi, *juan* 30, p. 398; quoted in *ZGWP*, vol. 10, p. 53. (The *juan* number is erroneously given as 49 on p. 62.)

36. Wang Shizhen [1760] n.d., *juan* 3, 11a. Partial translation appears in Liu 1975, p. 44. For a slightly different translation of the same passage, see Lynn 1975, p. 242.

37. The Chan-poetry analogy in traditional Chinese poetics is complex and multidimensional; see Lynn 1987b.

38. Dante, *Il convito*, III, 4; quoted in Qian Zhongshu 1979, vol. 2, p. 408. [The quotation is actually Qian's abbreviated paraphrase of a longer passage from lines 34–39: "E dico che se defetto fia nelle *mie rime*, ciò è nelle mei parole . . . di ciò è da biasimare la debiletà dell'intelletto e la *cortezza del nostro parlare*, lo quale dal pensiero è vinto" (*Tutte le opere di Dante Alighieri*, edited by E. Moore and P. Toynbee [Oxford: University Press, 1904], p. 275): "And I say that if the defect is in my rhymes, that is, in my words . . . for this are to blame the weakness of the intellect and the abruptness of our speech: 'blame wit and words,' which are overpowered by the thought" (*The Banquet of Dante Alighieri*, translated by Elizabeth Price Sayer [London: George Routledge and Sons, 1887], p. 110).]

39. Spenser 1930, canto II, vii. I am indebted to my daughter Sarah for calling my attention to this passage.

40. Marlowe, *Tamburlaine the Great*, part I, act 1, scene 5, lines 98–110.

41. Swinburne 1908, p. 2.

42. Shakespeare, Sonnet 18.

43. Shakespeare, Sonnet 106.

44. Tenth Congress of the International Comparative Literature Association, New York, 1982; see Liu 1985.

45. Aldridge 1982, p. 5.

46. Mallarmé 1945, p. 368; see Yu 1978a, p. 310.

47. Barbier 1971, p. 201; Michaud 1965, p. 194; Liu 1975, p. 56.

48. *Zhuang Zi yinde*, 7/3/1; previously quoted in Liu 1975, p. 56.
49. Eliot 1944, p. 12.
50. Ibid.
51. Ibid., p. 21.
52. Esslin 1961, p. 44.
53. Ibid., pp. 44, 46.
54. Merrell 1985, p. 189.
55. Snyder 1983. Cf. Jameson 1981, p. 13, where the axe handle is mentioned as part of a "Chinese proverb" and given a Marxist twist, as a symbol of a stronger interpretation that can overthrow an existing one.

### Chapter 3. The Poetics of Paradox

1. Chen Shou 1973, *Wei shu, juan* 21, p. 609. I am indebted to Professor Hans Frankel for locating the source of this anecdote.
2. Kroll 1985, p. 29.
3. Gao Heng 1956, p. 95.
4. *Zhuang Zi yinde*, 5/2/43.
5. Xuan Ying [1721] 1867, *juan* 2, 10b. This passage is also quoted in Wang Xianqian [1909] n.d., *juan* 1, 7a.
6. Cf. Graham 1981, p. 54. *Zhaoshi* (which can mean either "Mister/Master Zhao" or "the Zhao family/clan") here surely refers to an individual, the Zhao Wen mentioned in the next sentence, and should be rendered "Master Zhao." Graham, however, takes it in the other sense: "the Chao [Zhao]."
7. This interpretation is based on the commentaries of Xuan Ying and Wang Xianqian. See note 5 above.
8. Wang Liqi [1952] 1968, p. 105.
9. Kukai 1975, p. 128. Cf. Bodman 1978, p. 365.
10. Kukai 1975, p. 133. Cf. Bodman 1978, p. 382.
11. Kukai 1975, p. 139. Cf. Bodman 1978, p. 398.
12. Wang Wei, *juan* 7, 4b.
13. See Yu 1980, pp. 163–164.
14. Wang Wei, *juan* 19, 14b. Quoted in Qian Zhongshu 1979, vol. 2, p. 457.
15. Li Bai, *juan* 19, 15a.
16. Liu Changqing, *juan* 3, 6b.
17. Cheng 1982, p. 170.

18. Ibid., p. 171.
19. Jiaoran in *ZGWP*, vol. 2, p. 83. This passage is from Jiaoran's "General Preface" (*zongxu*), which does not always appear in editions of the *Shishi*; for instance, it does not appear in the one contained in *Lidai shihua* (He Wenhuan [1740] n.d.). Cf. Robertson 1972, pp. 338–339.
20. Jiaoran, p. 85; He Wenhuan [1740] n.d., 2b.
21. Jiaoran, p. 97. This passage is not in He Wenhuan [1740] n.d.
22. Jiaoran, p. 89; He Wenhuan [1740] n.d., 7a.
23. Jiaoran, pp. 89–90. This passage is not in He Wenhuan [1740] n.d.
24. Xiao Tong, *juan* 19, 2a.
25. See Yu 1983 and chapter 4 below.
26. See Huang Jie [1928] 1975, p. 11. For a translation and a modern interpretation, see Frankel 1964, pp. 9–10.
27. Wang Wei, *juan* 8, 2a.
28. *QTS*, p. 1443. The third line in this edition has a variant reading *niao* ("birds") instead of *ming* ("cries"), which would result in the translation ". . . beyond the apes and birds."
29. For a detailed description of this anthology, see Knechtges 1982.
30. For translations of this poem, see Waley 1946, p. 56; Watson 1971, p. 20; Liu and Lo 1975, pp. 30–31; Birrell 1982, pp. 38–39.
31. Sui Shusen 1958, p. 2.
32. The text is in Hong Xingzu, *juan* 8, 2a. For translation, see Hawkes [1959] 1962, p. 92.
33. Belpaire 1957.
34. Du Songbo [1976] 1978, pp. 416–423.
35. Giles 1923, p. 183; Belpaire 1957, p. 73; Yang and Yang 1963, p. 7; Yip 1969, pp. 280–281; Yu 1978b, p. 99.
36. Xiao Shuishun 1972, p. 15; Lynn 1983b, p. 177.
37. See note 35 and also Zhang 1983. Cf. Lynn 1975, p. 245, and Lynn 1983b, p. 177, where *fengliu* is interpreted as "the spirit of it."
38. *Cihai*, vol. 2, p. 3199.
39. Qian Zhongshu 1984, p. 92.
40. [Richard John Lynn's translation of this passage reads, "Not becoming attached to a single word / Completely get the spirit of it." The following involves a somewhat different interpreta-

tion: "I had previously translated this couplet as 'Without writing down a single word, / Completely get the spirit of it' " (Lynn 1975, p. 245). Now I think that *zhuo* ought to be rendered in a more literal sense—"be attached to, be committed to"—since Sikong seems to be referring to the supraverbal state that overrides composition, which the poet experiences *before* the poem takes shape in words. The reader apparently experiences this kind of poetry in the same way—the meaning comes across in such a way that one is unconscious of the words involved; the reader also remains "unattached" to them. See Lynn 1983b, p. 177 n. 91.]

41. Sikong Tu in He Wenhuan [1740] n.d., 3a.
42. For the two readings, see Guo Shaoyu 1965, p. 21, and Zu Baoquan 1966, p. 42.
43. *Zhuang Zi yinde*, 4/2/15. Cf. Graham 1981, p. 151.
44. See note 42.
45. Sikong Tu in He Wenhuan [1740] n.d., 5a–5b. A slightly different translation has appeared in Liu 1975, p. 35, where the reasons are given for translating various words in certain ways.
46. See Chaves 1976, pp. 114–127.
47. See Liu 1975, p. 103.
48. Ouyang Xiu, 6a. Cf. Chaves 1976, p. 110.
49. Chaves 1976, p. 113.
50. The most extensive study in English of the influence of Chan on Chinese poetics—including that of the Song period—is Lynn 1987b.
51. *ZGWP*, vol. 3, p. 205; Guo Shaoyu 1956, p. 235.
52. *ZGWP*, vol. 3, p. 202; Guo Shaoyu 1956, p. 235.
53. *ZGWP*, vol. 3, p. 217.
54. Rickett 1978, p. 107.
55. *ZGWP*, vol. 4, p. 257; Luo Genze 1961, p. 151. Cf. Schmidt 1976, pp. 47–48.
56. Jiang Kui in He Wenhuan [1740] n.d., 3b.
57. Ibid., 4a–4b. Cf. Lin 1983, p. 303.
58. Zhang Jian, introduction to *ZGWP*, vol. 4, p. 44.
59. See Smith 1968.
60. Jiang Kui in He Wenhuan [1740] n.d., 4a–4b. This text differs from the version reprinted in Xia Chengtao [1961] 1972, which

has one sentence missing and which is punctuated differently; the punctuation here follows Guo Shaoyu 1956, p. 229.

61. See note 23.
62. *Zhuang Zi yinde*, 1/1/3. Cf. Graham 1981, p. 43.
63. Fang Xuanling, p. 1289. Cf. Mather 1976, p. 389.
64. *Zhuang Zi yinde*, 55/21/2.
65. See Guo Shaoyu 1956, pp. 235–238, and Lynn 1983a.
66. For the text, see Guo Shaoyu 1962, pp. 23–24. A slightly different translation has appeared in Liu 1975, p. 39.
67. A detailed survey of the dissenters and followers that Yan's views called forth, with analyses of all the positions involved, appears in Lynn 1983b.
68. [In a letter to his maternal uncle, Wu Jingxian, Yan declares that "no work succeeds better than this one of mine at using Chan as an analogy for poetry." See Guo Shaoyu 1962, p. 234.]
69. Ibid., p. 10. For the various dimensions of the Chan-poetry analogy as it was used by Yan and others, see Lynn 1987b.
70. See Du Songbo [1976] 1978, pp. 424–428; Lynn 1983a, pp. 174–175; and Lynn 1987b.
71. See Lynn 1983b and Lynn 1987b.
72. See Lynn 1987a.
73. Wang Ruoxu, *juan* 38, quoted in *ZGWP*, vol. 5, p. 31.
74. Gao Heng 1956, p. 100. Cf. Lau 1963, p. 106.
75. *ZGWP*, vol. 5, p. 172; Guo Shaoyu 1956, pp. 266–267.
76. *ZGWP*, vol. 7, p. 403.
77. Tao Qian, *juan* 2, 1a–2b. Cf. Hightower 1970, pp. 42–47, and Davis 1983, vol. 1, pp. 34–43.
78. *ZGWP*, vol. 7, p. 567.
79. See Lynn 1975, pp. 217–237; Lynn 1983a, pp. 317–328; and Lynn 1983b, pp. 159–162.
80. Xie Zhen, *juan* 1, 9a.
81. Ibid. For a somewhat different translation of this passage, see Lynn 1977, p. 4.
82. See Liu 1975, p. 125.
83. Xie Zhen, *juan* 4, 11b–12a.
84. Su Shi, *Dongpo ji, juan* 16, 10b. For a free paraphrase of the poem, see Watson 1965, p. 109.
85. Valéry 1958, p. 174.
86. Auden [1948] 1962, p. 22.

87. Yuan Hongdao 1935, p. 5; quoted in *ZGWP*, vol. 9, p. 640. A partial translation has appeared in Liu 1975, p. 81.

88. *ZGWP*, vol. 8, p. 26.

89. See Lynn 1975, pp. 222, 238–240.

90. *ZGWP*, vol. 10, p. 32.

91. The whole question of the talent-learning polarity in Chinese poetics has been examined in Lynn 1983b.

92. Wang Fuzhi, p. 2, in Ding Fubao 1963.

93. See Karlgren 1974, p. 5.

94. Wen Yiduo 1956, pp. 121–122.

95. This work is the [*Zengding*] *Guangyu ji* by Lu Yingyang (Ming), revised by Cai Fangbing (mid to later seventeenth century). See *SKZM*, *juan* 72, 8a–8b.

96. The translation has previously appeared in Liu 1982a, p. 32.

97. Wang Fuzhi, p. 19, in Ding Fubao 1963.

98. See Liu [1962] 1983, pp. 83–84; Liu 1975, pp. 43–45; Lynn 1975, pp. 240–254.

99. *ZGWP*, vol. 11, p. 427.

100. Yan Yu, in Guo Shaoyu 1962, p. 6.

101. For general discussion about the *ci*, see Liu 1974, pp. 1–5, 10–16; Chang 1980, pp. 1–25.

102. Zhang Yan, 4a, in Tang Guizhang [1934] 1967, vol. 1, *juan xia*.

103. Zhang Yan, 4b.

104. Ibid.

105. *QTS*, 1892.

106. Li Yu, 4a, in Tang Guizhang [1934] 1967, vol. 2.

107. Liu Tiren, 3a, in Tang Guizhang [1934] 1967, vol. 2.

108. Li Yimang 1981, p. 108. Cf. Fusek 1982, p. 121.

109. Wang Shizhen [1760] n.d., 1b, in Tang Guizhang [1934] 1967, vol. 2. The *locus classicus* for the last sentence is the opening passage of the *Xun Zi* (fourth century B.C.); see *Xun Zi yinde*, 1/1/1. Cf. Watson 1963, p. 15.

110. Shen Qian, 2a, in Tang Guizhang [1934] 1967, vol. 2.

111. For translation and discussion of this lyric, see Liu 1974, pp. 19–20.

112. Liu Xizai [1873] 1964, *juan* 4, 9a; also in Tang Guizhang [1934] 1967, vol. 11, 10b.

113. See Liu 1975, p. 44.

114. Wang Guowei, 1b, in Tang Guizhang [1934] 1967, vol. 12; also in Xu Tiaofu 1955, p. 3. Cf. Rickett 1977, p. 42.
115. Rickett 1978, p. 107.
116. This usage has been pointed out in Rao Zongyi (Jao Tsung-i) 1955.
117. Zhu Guangqian 1980.
118. Zhang Wenxun 1983, p. 7.
119. Shakespeare, Sonnet 85.
120. Keats 1949, p. 365.
121. Bai Juyi, *juan* 12, 10b.
122. Qian Zhongshu 1979, vol. 2, p. 450.
123. Carlyle 1937, pp. 218–219.
124. Valéry 1958, p. 177. For other similarities between Yan Yu and Mallarmé, Claudel, and Valéry, see Qian Zhongshu 1984, pp. 92–94.
125. Dufrenne 1963, p. 97.
126. Merleau-Ponty 1964, pp. 43–45.
127. Derrida 1978, p. 262.
128. Bruckner 1985, p. 3.

*Chapter 4. The Paradox of Interpretation*

1. Cf. Qian Zhongshu 1984, p. 90.
2. Bloom 1973, p. 95.
3. Holzman 1978, p. 33.
4. Karlgren 1974, pp. 254–255.
5. *Lunyu yinde*, 2/2/2.
6. *Meng Zi yinde*, 36/5a/4. Cf. Lau 1970, p. 142.
7. Yu 1983, especially pp. 401–402, 410.
8. Sun Xingyan, p. 552.
9. Dong Zhongshu, *juan* 3, 10b.
10. Zhang 1983.
11. Qian Zhongshu 1984, p. 119.
12. Tao Qian, *juan* 6, 7b. Cf. Davis 1983, vol. 1, p. 208.
13. Tao Qian, *juan* 2, 12a. Cf. Hightower 1970, p. 74; Davis 1983, vol. 1, p. 64.
14. Yan Wei in *QTS*, vol. 4, p. 2914.
15. Wen Tingyun, *juan* 7, 5a.
16. Jia Dao, *juan* 8, 2a.

17. Ouyang Xiu, 6a–6b, in He Wenhuan [1740] n.d.
18. See Wong 1980.
19. Ouyang Xiu, 7b, in He Wenhuan [1740] n.d.
20. See note 81 to chapter 3.
21. Xie Zhen, *juan* 1, 1a.
22. He Wenhuan [1740] n.d., *Kaosuo*, 21a (appendix to *Lidai shihua*).
23. See also Lynn 1987b.
24. Cited in Guo Shaoyu 1956, p. 235.
25. Ibid., p. 236.
26. Ibid.
27. Yan Yu in Guo Shaoyu 1962, p. 11. The same passage is translated slightly differently in Lynn 1975, p. 221; for instance, *can* is rendered "identify with [it]."
28. Ingarden 1973b, p. 126.
29. Ibid., pp. 29, 335, 349, 351.
30. Dufrenne 1973, p. 146.
31. Wang Fuzhi, 1b, in Ding Fubao 1963.
32. *Zhuang Zi yinde*, 4/2/29. Cf. Graham 1981, p. 53.
33. Ingarden 1973a, p. 392; cited in Iser 1978, p. 176.
34. Ingarden 1973b, p. 252.
35. Iser 1978, p. 178.
36. Ibid., p. 22.
37. Ibid., pp. 181–182.
38. Liu 1982a, pp. 5–6.
39. Ingarden 1973a, p. 392; cited in Iser 1978, p. 176.
40. For the term "metaphysical" in this context, See Liu 1975, chapter 1.
41. See Magliola 1984, p. 65.
42. See Liu 1967, especially chapter 1.
43. I owe this insight to my daughter Sarah.
44. Wang Wei, *juan* 7, 6b.
45. Marlowe, *Doctor Faustus*, act 5, scene 1, line 120; Shakespeare, *Macbeth*, act 1, scene 1, line 11; Donne, "The Indifferent," in Donne 1949, p. 12.
46. See Liu [1962] 1983, p. 106.
47. I have previously used this example in Liu 1967, p. 42.
48. See Liu 1974, pp. 143–144.
49. Tang Guizhang 1982, p. 200.

50. See Hoy 1978, p. 22.
51. Li Bai, *juan* 31, 1a, 12a.
52. Wang Wei, *juan* 13, 7b.
53. See Liu 1981, p. 206.
54. Hong Xingzu, *juan* 2, 7a.
55. Wang Wei, *juan* 13, 8a.
56. For a somewhat different description of the intention of the text, see Hoy 1978, pp. 39–40.
57. Hightower 1968, pp. 41–44.
58. Li Bai, *juan* 2, 5a.
59. Ibid., *juan* 3, 29b.
60. Wang Wei, *juan* 13, 2a.
61. See *Tang shi xuan*, vol. 1, p. 118.
62. Wang Wei, *juan mo*, 29b–30a.
63. Liu 1982a, pp. 52–54.
64. *Meng Zi yinde*, 42/5b/8. Cf. Lau 1970, p. 158.
65. Wang Liqi [1952] 1968, p. 125.
66. Gadamer 1984, p. 273.
67. Hoy 1978, p. 138.
68. Gadamer 1984, p. 271.

*Afterword*

1. See note 1 to chapter 2.
2. [*Yuefu* originally was the name of a government department established during the Han dynasty (117 B.C.) that collected folk songs, created sacrificial music, and performed rites. The *yuefu shi* (music department poems) were works that related to these activities, especially folksongs gathered from the common people; this balladlike form became popular among literati and soon developed into a popular type of verse (*shi*).]
3. Wang Wei, *juan* 13, 4a.
4. Liu Zongyuan, *juan* 43, 14a–14b.
5. See Liu 1982a, pp. 4–12, 16–17.
6. Shelley 1880, vol. 3, p. 326.
7. Eliot 1944, p. 35.
8. Shelley 1880, vol. 3, p. 326.
9. Yu 1980, pp. 167–168.
10. Du Songbo [1976] 1978, p. 347.

11. Xu Tiaofu 1955, p. 1.
12. Keats, 1952, pp. 69, 227.
13. See Liu 1975, p. 36.
14. Keats 1952, p. 71.
15. See Liu 1975, p. 54.
16. Eliot 1932, pp. 10–11.
17. Ibid., p. 179.
18. Lu 1966, p. 24.
19. Allan 1974, p. 114.
20. Ibid., p. 74.
21. These and related issues are discussed in detail in Lynn 1983b.
22. See Liu 1975, p. 75.
23. Ye Xie, 8a.
24. Eliot 1932, p. 4.
25. Similar views were held by a number of Ming and Qing critics; see Lynn 1977.
26. Gardner 1949, pp. 31-32.

# Works Cited

*Works in Chinese*

Bai Juyi 白居易 (772–846). *Baishi Changqing ji* 白氏長慶集. In *SBBY*.

Ban Gu 班固 (32–92). *Han shu* 漢書. In *Ershiwu shi* 二十五史 (Kaiming ed.).

Cao Zhi (192–232). See Huang Jie [1928] 1975.

Chen Shou 陳壽 (223–297). 1973. *Sanguo zhi* 三國志. Commentary by Pei Songzhi 裴松之 (372–451). Beijing: Zhonghua shuju.

Chinese Academy of Social Sciences, Literature Institute. 1978. *Tang shi xuan* 唐詩選. 2 vols. Beijing: Renmin wenxue chubanshe.

*Chu ci.* See Hong Xingzu.

*Cihai* 辭海. 1969. Compiled by Cihai bianji weiyuanhui. 2 vols. Taibei: Zhonghua shuju.

Confucius. See *Lunyu yinde.*

Ding Fubao 丁福保, ed. [1915] n.d. *Lidai shihua xubian* 歷代詩話續編. Reprint. Taibei: Yiwen yinshuguan.

———, ed. 1963. *Qing shihua* 清詩話. Preface by Guo Shaoyu. Beijing: Zhonghua shuju.

Dong Zhongshu 董中舒 (176–104 B.C.). *Chunqiu fanlu* 春秋繁露. In *Siku quanshu zhenben bieji* 四庫全書珍本別集.

Du Songbo 杜松柏. [1976] 1978. *Chan xue yu Tang Song shi xue* 禪學與唐宋詩學. Reprint. Taibei: Liming wenhua shiye gongsi.

Duan Yucai 段玉裁 (1735–1815). *Shuowen jiezi zhu* 說文解字注 (by Xu Shen). In *GXJB*.

Fang Xuanling 房玄齡 (578–648) et al. *Jin shu* 晉書. In *Ershiwu shi* (Kaiming ed.).

Gao Heng 高亨. 1956. *Lao Zi zhenggu* 老子正詁. Beijing: Zhonghua shuju.

———. 1980. *Shijing jinzhu* 詩經今注. Shanghai: Guji chubanshe.

Guo Qingfan 郭慶藩. [1894] 1961. *Zhuang Zi jishi* 莊子集釋. Preface by Wang Xiangqian. Beijing: Zhonghua shuju.

Guo Shaoyu 郭紹虞 (1893–1984). 1956. *Zhongguo wenxuepiping shi* 中國文學批評史. Rev. ed. Shanghai: Xinwenyi chubanshe.

Guo Shaoyu, ed. 1962. *Canglang shihua jiaoshi* 滄浪詩話校釋 (by Yan Yu). Beijing: Renmin wenxue chubanshe.

——, ed. 1965. *Shipin jijie* 詩品集解 (by Sikong Tu). Hong Kong: Commercial Press.

*Han shu.* See Ban Gu.

He Jingming 何景明 (1483–1521). [1531] 1555. *He Dafu ji* 何大復集. Preface by Wang Tingxiang 王廷相. N.p.

He Wenhuan 何文煥, ed. [1740] n.d. *Lidai shihua* 歷代詩話. Reprint. Taibei: Yiwen yinshuguan.

Hong Xingzu 洪興祖 (1090–1155). *Chu ci buzhu* 楚辭補注. In *SBBY*.

Huang Jie 黃節 (1874–1935). [1928] 1975. *Cao Zijian shi zhu* 曹子建詩集. Reprint. Taibei: Heluo tushu chubanshe.

Huijiao 慧皎 (497–554). *Gao seng zhuan* 高僧傳. In *Haishan xianguancongshu* 海山仙舘叢書.

*I Ching.* See *Yi Jing*.

Jao Tsung-i. See Rao Zongyi 1955.

Ji Yun 紀昀 (1724–1805) et al., eds, [1782] 1969. *Siku quanshu zongmu* 四庫全書總目. 10 vols. Reprint. Taibei: Yiwen yinshuguan.

Jia Dao 賈島 (777–841). *Changjiang ji* 長江集. In *SBBY*.

Jiang Kui 姜夔 (ca. 1155–1221). *Baishi Daoren shishuo* 白石道人詩說. In He Wenhuan [1740] n.d. See also Xia Chengtao [1961] 1972.

Jiaoran 皎然 (730–799). *Shishi* 詩式. In He Wenhuan [1740] n.d.; also in *ZGWP*, vol. 2.

*Jin shu.* See Fang Xuanling.

Ke Qingming 柯慶明 et al., eds. 1981. *Zhongguo wenxuepiping ziliao huibian* 中國文學批評資料彙編. 11 vols. Taibei: Chengwen chubanshe.

Kūkai (Konghai) 空海 (773–834). 1975. *Bunkyō hifuron (Wenjing mifulun)* 文鏡秘府論. Beijing: Renmin wenxue chubanshe.

*Lao Zi.* For editions, see Gao Heng 1956 and Yan Lingfeng 1954.

*Lao Zi zhushi* 老子注釋. 1977. Shanghai: Renmin chubanshe.

Li Bai 李白 (701–761). *Li Taibai shiji* 李太白詩集. In *SBBY*.

Li He 李賀 (790–816). 1958. *Li Changji geshi* 李長吉歌詩. Shanghai: Zhonghua shuju.

Li Mengyang 李夢陽 (1472–1529). [1531] 1602. *Kongtong ji* 空同集. Preface by Wang Tingxiang.

Li Yimang 李一氓, ed. 1981. *Huajian ji jiao* 花間集校. Rev. ed. Beijing: Renmin wenxue chubanshe.

Li Yu 李漁 (1611–1680). *Kuici guanjian* 窺詞管見. In Tang Guizhang [1934] 1967, vol. 2.

*Lie Zi.* For text, see Yang Bojun 1958.

Liu Changqing 劉長卿 (709–780). *Liu Suizhou ji* 劉隨州集. In *SBBY*.

Liu Tiren 劉體仁 (seventeenth century). *Qisongtang ciyi* 七頌堂詞繹. In Tang Guizhang [1934] 1967, vol. 2.

Liu Wenqi 劉文祺, ed. 1959. *Chunqiu Zuoshi zhuan jiuzhu shuzheng* 春秋左氏傳舊注疏証. Beijing: Chinese Academy of Science.

Liu Xie 劉勰 (ca. 465–ca. 522). *Wenxin diaolong* 文心雕龍. For editions, see Wang Liqi [1952] 1968 and Zhou Zhenfu 1981.

Liu Xizai 劉熙載 (1813–1881). [1873] 1964. *Yigai* 藝概. Printed 1927. Reprint. Taibei: Guangwen shuju. Also partially reprinted in Tang Guizhang [1934] 1967, vol. 11.

Liu Yan 劉弇 (1048–1102). *Longyun ji* 龍雲集. Excerpts quoted in *ZGWP*, vol. 3.

Liu Zongyuan 柳宗元 (773–819). *Liu Hedong quanji* 柳河東全集. In *SBBY*.

Lu Ji 陸機 (261–303). 1961. *Wenfu* 文賦. In *Wei Jin Nanbeichao wenxue shi cankao ziliao* 魏晉南北朝文學史參考資料. Hong Kong: Hongzhi shuju.

*Lunyu yinde* 論語引得. *HYSI*.

Luo Genze 羅根澤. 1961. *Zhongguo wenxuepiping shi* 中國文學批評史. Vol. 3. Beijing: Zhonghua shuju.

Ma Qichang 馬其昶. [1894] 1953. *Zhuang Zi gu* 莊子故. Printed 1905. Reprinted with commentary by Yan Fu 嚴復 (1853–1921) and preface by Zeng Keduan 曾克耑. N.p.

*Mencius.* See *Meng Zi yinde*.

*Meng Zi yinde* 孟子引得. *HYSI*.

Ouyang Jian 歐陽建 (d. A.D. 300). *Yan jinyi lun* 言盡意論. In Ouyang Xun 1965, Yan Kejun [1815] 1959, and *ZGWP*, vol. 1.

Ouyang Xiu 歐陽修 (1007–1072). *Liuyi shihua* 六一詩話. In He Wenhuan [1740] n.d.

Ouyang Xun 歐陽詢 (557–641). 1965. *Yiwen leiju* 藝文類聚. Beijing: Zhonghua shuju.

Peng Dingqiu 彭定求 (1647–1715) et al., eds. 1960. *Quan Tang shi* 全唐詩. Beijing: Zhonghua shuju.

Qian Qianyi 錢謙益 (1582–1664). *Muzhai youxue ji* 牧齋有學集. In *SBCK*; also in *ZGWP*, vol. 10.

Qian Zhongshu 錢鍾書. [1948] 1965. *Tanyi lu* 談藝錄. Shanghai: Kaiming. Reprint. Hong Kong: Longmen shudian.

———. 1979. *Guanzhui bian* 管錐編. 4 vols. Beijing: Zhonghua shuju.

———. 1984. *Yeshi ji* 也是集. Hong Kong: Guangjiaojing chubanshe.

*Quan Tang shi.* See Peng Dingqiu et al. 1960.

Rao Zongyi (Jao Tsung-i) 饒宗頤. 1955. "Renjian cihua pingyi 人間詞話平議." *Rensheng zazhi* 人生雜誌, nos. 115−116 (Hong Kong), pp. 12−14, 11−12.

Shao Yong 邵雍 (1011−1077). 1066. *Yichuan jirang ji* 伊川擊壤集. Ming ed.

Shen Qian 沈謙 (1620-1670). *Tianci zashuo* 填詞雜說. In Tang Guizhang [1934] 1967, vol. 2.

Shen Yue 沈約 (441−513). *Song Shu* 宋書. In *Ershiwu shi* (Kaiming ed.).

*Shi jing*. See Gao Heng 1980.

Sikong Tu. See Guo Shaoyu 1965 and Zu Baoquan 1966.

*Siku quanshu zongmu*. See Ji Yun et al. [1782] 1969.

*Song Shu*. See Shen Yue.

Su Shi 蘇軾 (1037−1101). *Dongpo qiji* 東坡七集. In *SBBY*.

Sui Shusen 隋樹森. 1958. *Gushi shijiushou jishi* 古詩十九首集釋. Hong Kong: Zhonghua shuju.

Sun Xingyan 孫星衍 (1753−1818). *Zhou yi jijie* 周易集解. In *CSJC*.

Tang Guizheng 唐圭璋, ed. [1934] 1967. *Cihua congbian* 詞話叢編. Reprint. Taibei: Guangwen shuju.

——— et al., eds. 1982. *Tang Song ci xuanzhu* 唐宋詞選注. Beijing: Beijing chubanshe.

*Tang shi xuan*. See Chinese Academy of Social Sciences 1978.

Tao Qian 陶潛 (365−427). *Jingjie xiansheng ji* 靖節先生集. In *SBBY*.

Wang Fuzhi 王夫之 (1619−1692). *Jiangzhai shihua* 薑齋詩話. In Ding Fubao 1963.

Wang Guowei 王國維 (1877−1927). *Renjian cihua* 人間詞話. In Tang Guizhang [1934] 1967, vol. 12; also see Xu Tiaofu 1955.

Wang Liqi 王利器. [1952] 1968. *Wenxin diaolong xinshu* 文心雕龍新書. Beijing: Centre franco-chinois d'études sinologiques. Reprint. Taibei: Chengwen chubanshe.

Wang Ruoxu 王若虛 (1174−1243). *Hunan xiansheng wenji* 滹南先生文集. Excerpts quoted in *ZGWP*, vol. 5.

Wang Shizhen 王士禎 (1634−1711). [1760] n.d. *Daijingteng shihua* 帶經堂詩話. Reprint. Shanghai: n.p.

———. *Huacao mengshi* 花草蒙拾. In Tang Guizhang [1934] 1967, vol. 2.

Wang Wei 王維 (701−761). *Wang Youcheng ji zhu* 王右丞集注. In *SBBY*.

Wang Xianqian 王先謙 (1842−1917). [1909] n.d. *Zhuang Zi jijie* 莊子集解. Shanghai: Saoye shanfang.

Wang Yuanhua 王元化. 1979. *Wenxin diaolong chuangzuolun* 文心雕龍創作論. Shanghai: Guji chubanshe.

Wang Zhongling 王鍾陵. 1983. "Guanyu yan yi zhi bian 關於言意之辯." *GDWL* 8:77–99.

Wen Tingyun 溫庭筠 (ca. 812–870). *Wen Feiqing ji* 溫飛卿集. In *SBBY*.

Wen Yiduo 聞一多 (1899–1946). 1956. *Gudian xinyi* 古典新義. Beijing: Guji chubanshe.

Wu Cheng 吳澄 (1249–1333). *Wu Wenzheng gong ji* 吳文正公集. Excerpts quoted in *ZGWP*, vol. 7.

Xia Chengtao 夏承燾, ed. [1961] 1972. *Baishi shi ci ji* 白石詩詞集. Reprint. Hong Kong: Commercial Press.

Xiao Shuishun 蕭水順. 1972. *Sikong Tu shipin yanjiu* 司空圖詩品研究. Taibei: Shida guowen yanjiu suo.

Xiao Tong 蕭統 (501–531), comp. *Wenxuan* 文選. In *SBBY*.

Xie Zhen 謝榛 (1495–1575). *Siming shihua* 四溟詩話. In Ding Fubao [1915] n.d.

Xu Shen 許慎 (30–124). See Duan Yucai.

Xu Tiaofu 徐調浮, ed. 1955. *Jiaozhu Renjian cihua* 校注人間詞話. Beijing: Zhonghua shuju.

Xuan Ying 宣穎. [1721] 1867. *Nanhua jing jie* 南華經解. N.p.

*Xun Zi yinde* 荀子引得. *HYSI*.

Yan Kejun 嚴可均 (1762–1843). [1815] 1959. *Quan shanggu Sandai Qin Han Sanguo Liuchao wen* 全上古三代秦漢三國六朝文. Reprint. Beijing: Zhonghua shuju.

Yan Lingfeng 嚴靈峰. 1954. *Lao Zi zhangju xinbian* 老子章句新編. Taibei: Zhonghua wenhua chuban shiye weiyuanhui.

Yan Yu 嚴羽 (ca. 1195–ca. 1245). See Guo Shaoyu 1962.

Yang Bojun 楊柏峻. 1958. *Lie Zi jishi* 列子集釋. Beijing: Chinese Academy of Science.

Yang Xiong 楊雄 (53 B.C.–A.D. 18). *Fa yan* 法言. In *CSJC*.

Ye Xie 葉燮 (1627–1703). *Yuan shi* 原詩. In Ding Fubao [1915] n.d.

*Yi Jing* (*Zhou Yi*). See Sun Xingyan.

Yuan Haowen 元好問 (1190–1257). See *ZGWP*, vol. 5.

Yuan Hongdao 袁宏道 (1568–1610). 1935. *Yuan Zhonglang quanji* 袁中郎全集. Shanghai: Shijie shuju.

Yuan Xingpei 袁行霈. 1979. "Wei Jin xuanxue zhong di yan yi zhi bian yu Zhongguo gudai wenyi lilun 魏晉玄學中的言意之辯與中國古代文藝理論." *GDWL* 1:125–147.

Yuan Zongdao 袁宗道 (1568–1610). 1935. *Bai Su zhai leigao* 白蘇齋類稿. Shanghai: Shanghai zazhi.

Yuanwu 園悟. [1128] 1969. *Biyan lu* 碧巖錄. Reprinted 1305. In *Chan xue dacheng* 禪學大成, vol. 1. Taibei: Zhonghua fojiao wenhua guan.

Zhang Jian 張健. "Introduction." *ZGWP*, vol. 4.

Zhang Longxi 張隆溪. 1983. "Shi wu dagu 詩無達詁. "*Wenyi yanjiu* 文藝研究 4:13–17.

Zhang Wenxun 張文勛. 1983. "Lao Zhuang di meixue sixiang jiqi yingxiang 老莊的美學思想及其影響." *GDWL* 8:1–23.

Zhang Yan 張炎 (1248–1320). *Ci yuan* 詞源. In Tang Guizhang [1934] 1967, vol. 1.

Zhang Zhu 張翥 (1285–1364). *Wuxi ji* 午溪集. Excerpts quoted in *ZGWP*, vol. 7.

Zhao Nanxing 趙南星 (1550–1627). *Zhao Zhongyi gong shiwen ji* 趙忠毅公詩文集. Excerpts quoted in *ZGWP*, vol. 9.

*Zhongguo wenxuepiping ziliao huibian*. See Ke Qingming et al. 1981.

Zhou Chi 周馳. Preface to *Biyan lu*. See Yuanwu.

Zhou Zhenfu 周振甫, ed. 1981. *Wenxin diaolong zhushi* 文心雕龍注釋. Beijing: Renmin chubanshe.

Zhu Guangqian 朱光潛. 1980. *Zhu Guangqian wenxue meixue lunwen xuanji* 朱光潛文學美學論文集. Changsha: Hunan renmin chubanshe.

Zhuang Zi. For text, see *Zhuang Zi yinde*. For commentaries, see Guo Qingfan [1894] 1961, Ma Qichang [1894] 1953, Wang Xianqian [1909] n.d., and Xuan Ying [1721] 1867.

*Zhuang Zi yinde* 莊子引得. *HYSI*.

Zu Baoquan 祖保泉. 1966. *Sikong Tu shipin zhushi* 司空圖詩品注釋. Hong Kong: Commercial Press.

*Zuo zhuan*. See Liu Wenqi 1959.

*Works in Western Languages*

Aldridge, A. Owen. 1982. "East-West Resonances in New York." *TR* 13 (no. 1): 1–11.

Allan, Mowbray. 1974. *T. S. Eliot's Impersonal Theory of Poetry*. Lewisburg, Pa.: Bucknell University Press.

Auden, W. H. [1948] 1962. *The Dyer's Hand and Other Essays*. Reprint. New York: Random House.

Barbier, Carl Paul, ed. 1971. *Documents Stéphane Mallarmé*. Vol. 3. Paris: Nizet.

Belpaire, Bruno. 1957. *T'ang Kien Wen Tse*. Paris: Editions universitaires.

Birch, Cyril, ed. 1965. *An Anthology of Chinese Literature*. Vol. 1. New York: Grove Press.

Birrell, Anne, trans. 1982. *New Songs from a Jade Terrace*. London: Allen and Unwin.

Bloom, Harold. 1973. *The Anxiety of Influence*. New York: Oxford University Press.

Bodman, Richard. 1978. "Poetics and Prosody in Medieval China: A Study and Translation of Kūkai's *Bunkyō hifuron*." Ph.D. diss., Cornell University.

Brooks, Cleanth. 1947. *The Well-wrought Urn*. New York: Renal and Hitchcock.

Bruckner, D.J.R. 1985. "Forging a New Dramatic Language," *New York Times*, 7 July, sec. 2.

Carlyle, Thomas. 1937. *Sartor Resartus*. Edited by Charles Frederick Harrold. New York: Odyssey Press.

Chang, Chung-yuan. 1975. *Tao: A New Way of Thinking*. New York: Harper and Row.

Chang, Kang-i Sun. 1980. *The Evolution of Chinese Tz'u Poetry*. Princeton: Princeton University Press.

Chaves, Jonathan. 1976. *Mei Yao-ch'en and the Development of Early Sung Poetry*. New York: Columbia University Press.

Ch'en, Shih-hsiang, trans. 1965. "Essay on Literature." In Cyril Birch, ed., *An Anthology of Chinese Literature*, vol. 1, pp. 204–214. New York: Grove Press.

Cheng, Francois. 1982. *Chinese Poetic Writing*. Translated from the French by Donald A. Riggs and Jerome P. Seaton. Bloomington: Indiana University Press.

Ch'ien, Edward T. 1984. "The Conception of Language and the Use of Paradox in Buddhism and Taoism." *JCP* 11 (no. 4): 375–399.

Cleary, Thomas, and J. C. Cleary, trans. 1977. *The Blue Cliff Record*. Boulder, Colo.: Shambala.

Creel, Herrlee, G. 1983. "On the Opening Words of the *Lao-Tzu*." *JCP* 10 (no. 4): 299–329.

Davis, A. R. 1983. *T'ao Yuan-ming*. 2 vols. London: Cambridge University Press.

Derrida, Jacques. 1976. *Of Grammatology*. Translated by Gayatri Charkavorty Spivak. Baltimore: Johns Hopkins University Press.

———. 1978. *Writing and Difference*. Translated by Alan Bass. London: Routledge and Kegan Paul.

Donne, John. 1949. *The Poems of John Donne*. Edited Sir Herbert Grierson. London: Oxford University Press.

Dufrenne, Mikel. 1963. *Language and Philosophy*. Translated by Henry B. Veatch. Bloomington: Indiana University Press.

———. 1973. *The Phenomenology of Aesthetic Experience*. Translated by Edward Casy et al. Evanston, Ill.: Northwestern University Press.

Eliot, T. S. 1932. *Selected Essays*. New York: Harcourt, Brace.

———. 1944. *Four Quartets*. London: Faber and Faber.

Esslin, Martin. 1961. *The Theatre of the Absurd*. New York: Anchor Books.

Fang, Achilles, trans. [1951] 1965. "Rhymeprose on Literature: The *Wen-fu* of Lu Chi (A.D. 261–303)." *HJAS* 14: 527–566. Reprint. In John L. Bishop, ed., *Studies in Chinese Literature*, pp. 3–42. Cambridge: Harvard University Press.

Fokkema, D. W. 1978. "Chinese and Renaissance Artes Poeticae." *CLS* 15 (no. 2): 159–165.

Frankel, Hans H. 1964. Fifteen Poems by Ts'ao Chih: An Attempt at a New Approach." *Journal of the American Oriental Society* 84 (no. 1): 1–14.

Fusek, Lois, trans. 1982. *Among the Flowers: The Hua-chien chi*. New York: Columbia University Press.

Gadamer, Hans-Georg. 1984. *Truth and Method*. New York: Crossroad.

Gardner, Helen. 1949. *The Art of T. S. Eliot*. London: Cresset Press.

Giles, Herbert A. 1923. *A History of Chinese Literature*. New York: Appleton.

Graham, A. C., trans. 1960. *Lieh Tzu*. London: John Murray.

———, trans. 1981. *Chuang Tzu: The Inner Chapters*. London: Allen and Unwin.

Hansen, Chad. 1983. *Language and Logic in Ancient China*. Ann Arbor: University of Michigan Press.

Hawkes, David, trans. [1959] 1962. *Ch'u Tz'u: Songs of the South*. London: Oxford University Press. Reprint. Boston: Beacon Press.

Hightower, J. R. 1968. "T'ao Ch'ien's 'Drinking Wine Poems.' " In Tse-tsung Chow, ed., *Wen-lin: Studies in the Chinese Humanities*, pp. 3–44. Madison: University of Wisconsin Press.

———. 1970. *The Poetry of T'ao Ch'ien*. New York: Oxford University Press.

Hofstadter, Douglas H. 1979. *Godel, Escher, Bach*. New York: Basic Books.

Holzman, Donald. 1978. "Confucius and Ancient Chinese Literary Criticism." In Adele Rickett, ed., *Chinese Approaches to Literature from Confucius to Liang Ch'i-ch'ao*, pp. 21–42. Princeton: Princeton University Press.

Hoy, David Couzzens. 1978. *The Critical Circle*. Berkeley: University of California Press.

Ingarden, Roman. 1973a. *The Cognition of the Literary Work of Art*. Translated by Ruth Ann Crowley and Kenneth P. Olson. Evanston, Ill.: Northwestern University Press.

———. 1973b. *The Literary Work of Art*. Translated by George G. Grabowicz. Evanston, Ill.: Northwestern University Press.

Iser, Wolfgang. 1978. *The Act of Reading*. Baltimore: Johns Hopkins University Press.

Jameson, Fredric. 1981. *The Political Unconscious*. Ithaca, N.Y.: Cornell University Press.

Kao, Kung-yi, and Diane B. Obenchain. 1975. "Kung-sun Lung's Chih Wu Lun and the Semantics of Reference and Predication." *JCP* 2: 285–324.

Karlgren, Bernhard. 1972. *Grammata Serica Recensa*. Stockholm: Museum of Far Eastern Antiquities.

———, trans. 1974. *The Book of Odes*. Stockholm: Museum of Far Eastern Antiquities.

Keats, John. 1949. *The Poems and Verses of John Keats*. Edited by John Middleton Murry. London: Eyre and Spottiswoode.

———. 1952. *The Letters of John Keats*. Edited by Maurice Buxton Forman. London: Oxford University Press.

Kenner, Hugh. 1975–1976. "The Poetics of Error." *TR* 6 (no. 2) and 7 (no. 1), pp. 89–97.

Knechtges, David, R. 1981. *The Han shu Biography of Yang Xiong*. Tempe: Arizona State University, Center for Asian Studies.

———, trans. 1982. *Wen Xuan, or Selections of Refined Literature*. Vol. 1. Princeton: Princeton University Press.

Kroll, Paul. 1985. "The Flight from the Capital and the Death of Precious Consort Yang." *T'ang Studies* 3: 25–53.

Lau, D. C., trans. 1963. *Lao Tzu: Tao Te Ching*. Baltimore: Penguin Books.

———, trans. 1970. *Mencius*. Baltimore: Penguin Books.

———, trans. 1982. *Tao Te Ching*. Hong Kong: Chinese University Press.

Lin, Shuen-fu. 1983. "Chiang K'uei's Treatises on Poetry and Calligraphy." In Susan Bush and Christian Murck, eds., *Theories of the Arts in China*, pp. 93–316. Princeton: Princeton University Press.

Lindenberger, Herbert. 1984. "Toward a New History in Literary Study." *Profession*, pp. 16–23.

Liu, James J. Y. [1962] 1983. *The Art of Chinese Poetry*. Reprint. Chicago: University of Chicago Press.

———. 1967. *The Chinese Knight-Errant*. Chicago: University of Chicago Press.

———. 1974. *Major Lyricists of the Northern Sung*. Princeton: Princeton University Press.

———. 1975. *Chinese Theories of Literature*. Chicago: University of Chicago Press.

———. 1979. *Essentials of Chinese Literary Art*. North Scituate, Mass.: Duxbury Press.

———. 1981. Review of *China and the West: Comparative Literature Studies*, William Tay et al., eds., *CLS* 18 (no. 2): 201–207.

———. 1982a. The Interlingual Critic. Bloomington: Indiana University Press.

———. 1982b. "A Note on Po Chü-yi's *'Tu Lao Tzu'* " *CLEAR* 4 (no. 2): 243–244.

———. 1985. "The Paradox of Poetics and the Poetics of Paradox." In *Proceedings of the Tenth Congress of the International Comparative Literature Association*. New York: Garland Publishing.

Liu, Wu-chi, and Irving Yucheng Lo, eds. 1975. *Sunflower Splendor: Three Thousand Years of Chinese Poetry*. New York: Doubleday.

Lu, Fei-pai. 1966. *T. S. Eliot: The Dialectical Structure of His Theory of Poetry*. Chicago: University of Chicago Press.

Lynn, Richard John. 1975. "Orthodoxy and Enlightenment: Wang Shih-chen's Theory of Poetry and Its Antecedents." In William Theodore de Bary, ed. *The Unfolding of Neo-Confucianism*, pp. 217–69. New York: Columbia University Press.

———. 1977. "Tradition and the Individual: Ming and Ch'ing Views of Yüan Poetry." *Journal of Oriental Studies* 15: 1–19.

———. 1983a. "Alternate Routes to Self-Realization in Ming Theories of Poetry." In Susan Bush and Christian Murck, eds., *Theories of the Arts in China*, pp. 317–340. Princeton: Princeton University Press.

———. 1983b. "The Talent-Learning Polarity in Chinese Poetics: Yan Yu and the Later Tradition." *CLEAR* 5: 157–184.

————. 1987a. Review of J. Timothy Wixted, *Poems on Poetry: Literary Criticism of Yuan Hao-Wen (1190–1257)*. *HJAS* 47 (no. 2): 694–713.

————. 1987b. "The Sudden and the Gradual in Chinese Poetry Criticism: An Examination of the Ch'an-Poetry Analogy." In Peter N. Gregory, ed., *Sudden and Gradual: Approaches to Enlightenment in Chinese Thought*, pp. 381–427. Honolulu: University Press of Hawaii.

Magliola, Robert. 1984. *Derrida on the Mend*. West Lafayette, Ind.: Purdue University Press.

Mallarmé, Stéphane. 1945. *Oeuvres completes*. Edited by H. Mondor and G. Jean-Aubry. Paris: Gallimard.

Marlowe, Christopher. 1930. *Tamburlaine the Great*. Edited by Una Ellis–Fermor. London: Methuen.

————. 1949. *The Tragical History of Doctor Faustus*. Edited by Frederick S. Boas. London: Methuen.

Mather, Richard, trans. 1976. *Shih-shuo hsin-yü: A New Account of Tales of the World*. Minneapolis: University of Minnesota Press.

Merleau-Ponty, Maurice. 1962. *Phenomenology of Perception*. Translated by Colin Smith. London: Routledge and Kegan Paul.

————. 1964. *Signs*. Translated by Richard C. McCleary. Evanston, Ill.: Northwestern University Press.

Merrell, Floyd. 1985. *Deconstruction Reframed*. West Lafayette, Ind.: Purdue University Press.

Michaud, Guy. 1965. *Mallarmé*. Translated by Marie Collins and Bertha Humez. New York: New York University Press.

Miner, Earl. 1983. "The Grounds of Mimetic and Nonmimetic Art: The Western Sister Arts in a Japanese Mirror." In Richard Wendorf, ed., *Articulate Images: The Sister Arts from Hogarth to Tennyson*, pp. 70–97. Minneapolis: Minnesota University Press.

Peirce, Charles Sanders. 1932. *Collected Papers*. Edited by Charles Hartshorne and Paul Weiss. Vol. 2, *Elements of Logic*. Cambridge: Harvard University Press.

Plato. 1925. *Thirteen Epistles of Plato*. Translated by L. A. Post. London: Oxford University Press.

Pope, Alexander. 1962. "An Essay on Criticism." In Gay Wilson Allen and Henry Hayden Clark, eds., *Literary Criticism: Pope to Croce*. Detroit: Wayne State University Press.

Rickett, Adele, trans. 1977. *Wang Kuo-wei's Jen-chien Tz'u-hua: A Study in Chinese Literary Criticism*. Hong Kong: Hong Kong University Press.

———. 1978. "Method and Intuition: The Poetics of Huang T'ing-chien." In Adele Rickett, ed., *Chinese Approaches to Literature from Confucius to Liang Ch'i-ch'ao*, pp. 97–119. Princeton: Princeton University Press.

Robertson, Maureen. 1972. " . . . To Convey What Is Precious: Ssu-k'ung T'u's Poetics and the *Erh-shih-ssu Shih-p'in*." In David C. Buxbaum and Frederick W. Mote, eds., *Transition: Chinese History and Culture* (Festschrift Hsiao Kung-ch'üan), pp. 323–357. Hong Kong: Cathay Press.

Saussure, Ferdinand de. 1974. *Course in General Linguistics*. Translated by Wade Baskin. London: Fontana.

Schmidt, J. D. *Yang Wan-Li*. 1976. Boston: Twayne Publishers.

Shakespeare, William. 1938. *Sonnets*. London: Lund Humphries.

Shelley, P. B. 1880. *The Works of Percy Bysshe Shelley*. Edited by Harry Buxton Forman. London: Reeves and Turner.

Shih, Vincent Y. C., trans. 1959. *The Literary Mind and the Craving of Dragons*. New York: Columbia University Press.

Smith, Barbara Herrnstein. 1968. *Poetic Closure: A Study of How Poems End*. Chicago: University of Chicago Press.

Snyder, Gary. 1983. *Axe handles*. San Francisco: North Point Press.

Spenser, Edmund. 1930. *The Fairie Queene*. London: J. M. Dent and Sons.

Swinburne, A. C. 1908. *The Age of Shakespeare*. London: Chatto and Windus.

Valéry, Paul. 1958. *The Art of Poetry*. Translated by Denise Folliot. New York: Pantheon Books.

Waley, Arthur, trans. 1946. *Chinese Poems*. London: Allen and Unwin.

Watson, Burton, trans. 1963. *Hsun Tzu: Basic Writings*. New York: Columbia University Press.

———, trans. 1965. *Su Tung-p'o: Selections from a Sung Dynasty Poet*. New York: Columbia University Press.

———, trans. 1968. *The Complete Works of Chuang Tzu*. New York: Columbia University Press.

———. 1971. *Chinese Lyricism: Shih Poetry from the Second to the Twelfth Century*. New York: Columbia University Press.

Wesling, Donald. 1980. "Methodological Implication of the Philosophy of Jacques Derrida for Comparative Literature." In John J. Deeney, ed., *Chinese-Western Comparative Literature: Theory and Strategy*, pp. 79–111. Hong Kong: The Chinese University Press.

Wimsatt, William K., and Cleanth Brooks. 1965. *Literary Criticism: A Short History*. New York: Alfred P. Knopf.

Wittgenstein, Ludwig. 1961. *Tractatus Logico-Philosophicus*. Translated by D. F. Pears and B. F. McGinnes. London: Routledge and Kegan Paul.

Wong, W. L. 1980. "Selections of Lines in Chinese Poetry-Talk Criticism: With a Comparison between the Selected Couplets and Matthew Arnold's 'Touchstones.' " In William Tay et al., eds., *China and the West: Comparative Literature Studies*, pp. 33–44. Hong Kong: Chinese University Press.

Wu, John C. H. 1967. *The Golden Age of Zen*. Taipei: National War College.

Wu, Kuang-ming. 1982. *Zhuang Tzu: World Philosopher at Play*. New York: Crossroad Publishing and Scholar Press.

Yang, Hsien-yi, and Gladys Yang, trans. 1963. "The Twenty-Four Modes of Poetry." *Chinese Literature* 7: 65–77.

Yeh, Michelle. 1983. "The Deconstructive Way: A Comparative Study of Derrida and Chuang Tzu." *JCP* 10 (no. 2): 95–126.

Yip, Wai-lim, trans. 1969. "Selections from 'The Twenty-Four Orders of Poetry.' " *Stony Brook* 3/4, pp. 280–287.

Yu, Pauline R. 1978a. "Chinese and Symbolist Poetic Theories." *Comparative Literature* 30 (no. 4): 291–312.

———. 1978b. "Ssu-kung T'u's *Shih-p'in*: Poetic Theory in Poetic Form." In Ronald C. Miao, ed., *Chinese Poetry and Poetics*, vol. 1, pp. 81–103. San Francisco: Chinese Materials Center.

———. 1980. *The Poetry of Wang Wei*. Bloomington: Indiana University Press.

———. 1983. "Allegory, Allegoresis, and the *Classic of Poetry*." *HJAS* 43, (no. 2): 377–412.

Zach, Erwin von, trans. 1939. *Yang Hsiung's Fa-yan (Worte strenger Ermahnung)*, Ein philosophischer Traktat aus dem Beginn der christlichen Zeitrechnung. *Sinologische Beiträge* 4, no. 1 (Batavia: Drukkerij Lux).

Zhang, Longxi. 1983. "Poetry Has No Direct Interpretation." Paper presented at the Sino-American Symposium on Comparative Literature, Beijing. For Chinese version, see above under Works in Chinese.

———. 1985. ''The *Tao* and the *Logos*: Notes on Derrida's Critique of Logocentrism.'' *Critical Inquiry* 11, (no. 3): 385–398.

# Index

absence (*wu*), 20–21, 136
Aldridge, A. Owen, 53
Allan, Mowbray, 127
allegory, 64–65, 96
ambiguity, 66, 109
aposioppesis, 92
archaism, 50, 79, 145n
Aristotle, 22, 25, 125
Auden, W. H., 81
axe handle, 39, 41, 55

Bai, Duke of, 14, 15, 48, 131
Bai Juyi (or Bo Juyi), 6–7, 92
*Baishi Daoren shishuo*, 47–48
Baoxi (Fuxi), 18, 24, 131
Beckett, Samuel, 55
Belpaire, Bruno, 66
*bian* (change), 128, 131
*bian* ("eloquence" or "discrimination"), 9, 43, 131
*biaoxian shi* (expressive poetry), 120, 131
*Biyan lu*, 35
blandness (*dan*), 69, 72, 146n
Bloom, Harold, 93
Bodhidharma, 34
*Book (Classic) of Changes (Yi Jing)*, 17, 25, 44, 58, 97, 137
*Book (Classic) of Poetry (Shi Jing)*, 20, 83, 95–98, 100, 108
*Book of Documents* or *Classic of History (Shu Jing)*, 26
Boya (zither player), 117
Brecht, Bertolt, xii
Brooks, Cleanth, 3
Bruckner, D.J.R., 93
Buddhism, xii, 7, 13–14, 24, 33–36, 49–50, 62, 70, 78, 83, 109, 123–124, 141n

Buddhist *sútras*, 7, 50
*Bunkyō hifuron (Wenjing mifu lun)*, 59

*cai* (talent), 128
*can (canshi)*, 101–102, 131, 154n
Cang Jie, 18, 24, 131
*Canglang shihua*, 75–76
Cao Cao, 56–57, 131
Cao Pi, 56–57, 92, 131
Cao Zhi, 56–57, 63–64, 131
Carlyle, Thomas, 92
Cazalis, Henri, 126
Chan School of Buddhism, 14, 34–36, 48–49, 51, 60–61, 66–67, 70–71, 75–77, 101, 123–124, 131, 141n, 147n, 150n, 151n
Chang Chung-yuan, 23
Chaves, Jonathan, 69
Chen Shou, 56
Chen Yi, 78, 131
Chen Zi'ang, 102, 131
Ch'en Shih-hsiang, 55
*chenzhuo tongkuai*, 86, 131
Chu, King of, 64, 131
*chuanxin* (mind-to-mind-transmission), 34, 131
*chuangxin* (original innovation), 128, 131
*ci* (lyrics), 87–91, 121, 132, 152n
*Ci yuan*, 87
Claudel, Paul, 153n
concretization, 104
Confucianism, 17, 24–29, 35–36, 94–100, 108, 145n
Confucius, 4, 17, 25–29, 35, 37, 47–48, 95–97, 100, 104
Confucius (fictional), 10, 14–15, 75
*congrong bupo*, 86–132

conventionist view of language, 28–29

Cui Hao, 84, 132

Dahui, 35, 132
Dai Fugu, 101, 132
Dai Kui, 74, 132
*dan* (blandness), 69, 72
Dante, 51–52, 96, 147n
Dao (Tao), 5–6, 8, 11–13, 18, 22, 25, 28, 36–37, 60, 63, 75, 106, 124, 126
Daoism, xii, 4, 8, 13–14, 20, 22–23, 25, 33–34, 36, 61, 66, 70, 108, 124
Daoist view of language, 15, 21, 23
deconstruction, 21, 25
Derrida, Jacques, 4, 6, 11, 15, 20–23, 25, 93, 143n
*Dharma*, 35
*Diamond Sutra*, 50
diectic conception of language, xii
Dong Zhongshu, 97–98
Donne, John, 109
Du Fu, 49–50, 70, 78, 85–86, 102
Du Songbo, 66, 123
Dufrenne, Mikel, 92, 103

Eliot, T. S., 53–54, 123–124, 126–127, 129–130
Empson, William, 109
enlightenment (*wu*), 48–51, 60, 77, 79
Epimenides, 6
*Ershisi shipin*, 66
Esslin, Martin, 55
etymology of Chinese characters, 16–20
eye (key word), 70–71

*fan an* ("reversing previous opinions"), 31, 145n
Fang Wen, 50, 132
Faustus, 108
feminine principle, 21
*fengliu* ("wind-flow"), 67, 70, 149n
Fenollosa, Ernest, 19–23
Fish, Stanley, 28
fish trap (parable of), 11, 22, 48–49

flavor (or taste) (*wei*), 14, 46, 48, 57–58, 71–72, 78–79, 82, 125, 127, 136, 146n
fore-structures, 107
four interpretive phases of a literary work (lexical, syntactic, referential, intentional), 108–116
Freud, Sigmund, xii
*fu* (prose poem), 120, 132, 145n
Fuxi (Baoxi), 18, 23, 132

Gadamer, Hans-Georg, 117–118
Gao Heng, 8
Gao Zimian, 70
*gaomiao* (lofty marvelousness), 72, 132
Gardner, Helen, 130
*gāthā* (*jie*), 34
*gelü* (norms and rules), 128, 132
Giles, H. A., 66–67
*gong'an* (public cases), 34, 60, 132
Gongsun Chou, 27–28, 132
Gongsun Long, 29, 132
Graham, A. C., 8–9
graphocentrism, 16, 23
Guang, Reverend Master, 60
*Guangyu ji*, 84, 152n
Guanxiu (monk), 79, 132
Guo Shaoyu, 67, 75, 101
Guo Xiang, 132, 142n–143n

Han Yu, 85–132
Hansen, Chad, 5, 26
hare snare; *see* rabbit snare
He Jingming, 49, 51, 79
He Ning, 90, 132
He Wenhuan, 100
He Youwen, 78, 132
heart/mind (*xin*), 29–31, 37
Hegel, Georg, 33
Heidegger, Martin, 6, 20, 107
hermeneutic circle, 98–99, 108–116, 130
Hightower, J. R., 113
historical relativism, 116–118
historicism, 116–118

historico-biographico-tropological approach, 96–97
Holzman, Donald, 95
Homer, 50
Hou Ying (knight-errant), 107, 132
Hoy, David Couzzens, 118
*Huajian ji*, 90, 132
Huang Tingjian, 70–71, 88, 91, 102, 133
Huijiao, 34

indeterminacy of meaning, 103–112
Ingarden, Roman, 102–108
intentional phase of interpretation, *see* four interpretive phases of a literary work
intentionalism, 95–98, 103, 112–115, 155n
intersubjectivity, 101–102
Ionesco, Eugene, 54
Iser, Wolfgang, 104–107

Japanese pronunciation of Chinese characters (*on* and *kun*), 19
Jia Dao, 99
Jian, Prince, 14, 133
Jiang Kui, 47–48, 60, 72–75, 87
Jiangxi School of poetry, 70, 133
Jiaoran, 62–65, 74, 149n
*jie (gāthā)*, 34, 133
Jing Ke (knight-errant), 107, 133
*jing* (scene), 124
*jing* (world), 122, 124
*jingjie* (world), 91, 97, 127, 133

Kāśyapa, 4, 33–34
Keats, John, 92, 125–126
Kenner, Hugh, 20
*koan* (public cases), 34, 60, 132
*kong* (empty = śūnyatā), 123, 133
Kroll, Paul, 57
Kūkai (Kōbō Daishi), 59

Lacan, Jacques, 21
Langland, William, 130
langue-parole dichotomy, 6, 103
Lao Zi (*Lao Zi*), 4–9, 11, 13, 15–16, 21–25, 28, 33–35, 58, 78, 92, 133
Lau, D. C., 5
*Lebenswelt*, 103, 122
lexical phase of a literary work, *see* four interpretive phases of a literary work
*li* (reason/principles), 75, 133
Li Bai (or Li Bo), 60, 71, 79, 86, 88, 102–103, 111–114
Li He, 47
Li Mengyang, 49–51, 79
Li Quyan, 70, 133
Li Shan, 40, 64, 133
Li Yu (Houzhu), 89–90, 133
Li Yu (Liweng), 89, 126, 133
Li Zhiyi, 70, 133
liar paradox, 6
Lie Yukou, 14, 133
*Lie Zi*, 14, 48
Lindenberger, Herbert, xii
*Lisao*, 85, 133
Liu Changqing, 61
Liu Tiren, 89–91
Liu Xicai, 90
Liu Xie, 8, 18, 22, 24, 43, 45, 58–59, 75, 80, 117, 128
Liu Yan, 36–37
Liu Zongyuan, 122–123, 133
logocentrism, 15, 17, 20–26, 82
logographs or logograms, 18
Logos, 22; identification with God, 25
Lu, Fei-pai, 126–127
Lu Ji, 22, 24, 33, 38–42, 46, 51, 55, 71
Lu Yingyang, 152n
Lu Zhaolin, 102
Luo Binwang, 102, 133
Lynn, Richard John, 67, 85, 149n–150n
lyric poetry defined, 120–121

Ma Qichang, 11–12
*Macbeth*, 108
Magliola, Robert, 11, 13, 22–23
Mallarmé, Stéphane, 53–54, 126, 153n

Marlowe, Christopher, 52–53
Marx, Karl, xii, 148n
masculine principle, 21
Mauclair, Camille, 53–54
"meaning beyond words," 30, 45–
    46, 58–60, 62, 69, 75, 78–87, 91–93
Mei Yaochen, 69, 71–72, 133
Mencius, 27, 29, 46, 95–100, 116–117
Meng Haoran, 86
Merleau-Ponty, Maurice, 27, 93
Merrell, Floyd, 55
meta-language, 7
metaphysics of origin, 24
metaphysics of presence, 20–21, 24
*miaowu* (miraculous awakening), 77,
    134
mimetic concept of art and litera-
    ture, 15, 106, 125
mimetic concept of language, xii,
    15, 23
mimetic concept of writing, 23–24
Miner, Earl, xii
*ming* (name), 26, 28, 32, 134, 144n
*Ming jia* (School of Names), 29, 134
moralism, 95–98
music, 46, 57–58, 70–71, 78, 82–83,
    92, 117

Nāgārjuna, 14
negative capability, 126
Neo-classicism, 45
Neo-Confucianism, 36, 45
Nietzsche, Friedrich, 118
*Nineteen Ancient Poems*, 62–64, 82, 84

object language, 7
object stratum, 105
origin, myth of, 22, 24
Ouyang Jian, 31–33, 39
Ouyang Xiu, 69, 71, 99

painting, 84
paradox of language: first form, 3–
    10, 27–28; second form, 10–15,
    25–31
*paramārtha-satya*, 33–34
Pei Di, 111, 134

Pei Songzhi, 56
Peirce, C. S., 16–17
Peng (fabulous bird), 74
Petrach, 53
phallocentrism, 21
phenomenology, 101–103
phonocentrism/phonologism, 15–
    16, 23–24, 29, 37
Pian (wheelwright), 10, 22, 40–41,
    45
*pianwen* (parallel prose), 44, 134
Ping, King of Chu, 15, 134
Plato, 15, 26
Platonic form, 26
plurisignation, 66, 109
poetic closure, 73–74
Pope, Alexander, 50
Pound, Ezra, 19–20, 22–23, 55
pragmatic context, 116
pragmatic view of literature, 36–37,
    145n
Pre-Socratics, 20
presence (*you*), 20–21, 24, 137
presence, myth of, 22, 24
provisional names, 11

*qi* (breath, vital force, spirit,
    pneuma, ether), 27–28, 134
Qian Qianyi, 50–51, 82–83
Qian Zhongshu, 5, 7, 40, 47, 67, 92,
    97, 147n
*qing* (feeling/nature), 103, 124, 134
*qingkong* (pure and ethereal), 87–88,
    134
*qu* (lyric songs or dramatic lyrics),
    121, 134
*qu* (meaning, interest, [inspired]
    mood, gusto), 75, 79, 82, 107, 134
Qu Yuan, 85, 107, 134

rabbit snare (parable of), 11, 34, 48–
    49
raft (parable of), 48–49, 51
rectification of names (Confucius/
    Xun Zi), 28
referent, 33
referential phase of interpretation,

*see* four interpretive phases of a
    literary work
Ren An, 27, 134
*Renjian cihua*, 91
representativist concept of lan-
    guage, 21–23
Rickett, Adele, 71, 91
Romantic movement, 125–126
Rossetti, W. M., 123
Ruan Ji, 107, 134
Russell, Bertrand, 7

Śākyamuni, 4, 33, 35, 141n
*samvriti-satya*, 34
*Sanguo zhi*, 56
*sanqu* (detached or "scattered"
    songs), 121, 135
*santao* ("scattered" suits), 121, 135
Sartre, Jean-Paul, 20, 54
Saussure, Ferdinand de, 6, 16–17,
    103
School of Names (*Ming jia*), 29
Seaton, Jerome, 61
*Sein* ("Being"), 6
Sengzhao, 33, 134
Shakespeare, William, 52–53, 92
Shao Yong, 45–47
Shelley, P. B., 122–124
Shen Qian, 90
Shen Quanqi, 102, 135
*shen* (intuition, spirit), 44, 107, 135
*shensi* (intuitive thought), 44, 80,
    135
Shen Yue, 146n
*shenyun* (spirit and tone), 85, 97, 135
Shepard, Sam, 93
*shi* (verse), 34, 87, 120–121, 135,
    155n
*Shi Jing*, see *Book (Classic) of Poetry*
*shi yan zhi*, 124, 135
*Shige*, 59, 135
Shih, Vincent, 45
*Shiji*, 85
*Shishi*, 62, 149n
*Shu Jing*, see *Book of Documents* or
    *Classic of History*
Shun (sage emperor), 124

*Shuowen jiezi*, 18
*shuqing shi* (lyric poetry), 120
*si* (thought), 44
signified, 33
signifier, 33
Sikong Tu, 45, 66–72, 79, 86, 150n
Sima Qian, 27, 85, 135, 144n
*Siming shihua*, 79
Six Scripts (*liushu*), 16, 133
*sizhi* (natural order of [intuitive]
    thought), 80, 135
Smith, Barbara Herrnstein, 28, 73
Song Qi, 88, 91, 135
Song Yu, 63–64, 74, 135
Song Zhiwen, 102, 135
*sous rature*, 6
Spenser, Edmund, 51
*su di (samvriti-satya)*, 34, 135
Su Shi, 81–82, 87, 102, 109, 113, 125
*śūnyatá (kong)*, 123, 133
Swinburne, A. C., 52–53
Symbolists, 126
synaesthesia, 72
Synder, Gary, 55
syntactic phase of interpretation, *see*
    four interpretive phases of a liter-
    ary work

Tao Qian (Tao Yuanming), 43, 46,
    58, 62, 78, 83–84, 92, 98, 107, 113
*taoran* ("molding and dyeing" =
    cultivation), 128, 135
*taoshu* (suite numbers), 121, 135
taste, *see* flavor
*Tripiṭaka*, 35
tropological approach, 96
tropological interpretation, 96, 98,
    100
Twofold Truth, Theory of, 33

Valery, Paul, 81, 92, 153n
Virgil, 50

Waley, Arthur, 20
Wang, Anshi, 87, 135
Wang Bi, 44
Wang Bo, 102

Wang Changling, 59–60, 62–63, 65
Wang Fuzhi, 83–85, 103, 107
Wang Guowei, 91, 122, 125
Wang Huizhi, 74, 135
Wang Ruoxu, 77–78
Wang Shizhen (Wang Yuanmei), 51, 136
Wang Shizhen (Wang Yuyang), 51, 85, 90–91, 136
Wang Wei, 60, 63–64, 71, 86, 111, 113, 115, 122–123
Wang Xiangqian, 148n
Wang Yuanhua, 44
Wang Zhongling, 26–27, 145n
Watson, Burton, 12, 144n
*Wei shu*, 56, 136
*wen* ("writing" or "pattern"), 18, 49, 72, 117, 136
Wen Tingyun, 99
Wen Tong, 125, 136
Wenbo Xuezhi, 73, 75, 136
*Wenfu*, 22, 38–42, 46, 55
*Wenjing mifu lun*, see *Bunkyō hifuron*
*Wenxin diaolong*, 8, 22, 58–59, 75, 80, 117
*Wenxuan*, 65
Wesling, Donald, 21–24
Wimsatt, W. K., 109
Wittgenstein, Ludwig, 48–49
*wu* (absence), 20–21, 136
*wu* (enlightenment), 48–51, 60, 77, 79. See also *wujing*
*wu* (thing), 26, 32–33, 125, 136
*wu wo zhi jing*, 122, 136
Wu Cheng, 78
Wu Jingxian, 151n
Wu Weiyeh, 83, 136
Wu Wenying, 87, 136
Wu Zhi, 57

*xiang* (image), 44
Xiao Shuishun, 66–67
Xiao Tong, 65
*xiaoling* (little airs), 86, 121, 136
*Xici zhuan* ("Commentary on the Appended Phrases"), 17–18, 25, 29, 97, 136
Xie Lingyun, 62, 136

Xie Zhen, 79–81, 83, 100
*xiju shi* (dramatic poetry), 120, 136
*xin* (heart/mind), 29, 31
*xinghui* (inspired encounter), 91, 136
*xingling* (native sensibility), 128, 136
*xingqing* (personal nature), 128, 137
*xingqu* (inspired mood), 76, 91, 97, 137
Xu Rui, 101, 137
Xu Shen, 18
Xuan Ying, 58, 148n
*xue* (learning), 77, 83, 128, 137
*Xun Zi*, 28, 32, 152n
*xushi shi* (narrative poetry), 120, 137

*yan* (language, spoken or written), 16, 26, 43, 137
*Yan* (word), 13, 26–27, 31–32, 44, 137
Yan Shu, 90, 137
Yan Wei, 99, 137
Yan Yu, 60, 75–80, 82, 86–87, 91–92, 101–103, 126, 128, 151n, 153n
Yang Hsien-yi and Gladys Yang, 66–67
Yang Jiong, 102, 137
Yang Wanli, 71–72, 137
Yang Xiong, 29–30
*yanxi* (following tradition), 128, 137
Ye Xie, 128–129
Yellow Emperor (Huang Di), 18, 133
*yi* (meaning), 25–28, 31–33, 44, 96, 137, 144n
*Yi Jing*, see *Book (Classic) of Changes*
*yixiang* (mental image), 44, 137
*yin* and *yang*, 58
Yip, Wai-lim, 66–67
*yiqu* (meaning and mood), 87, 137
Yiya (or Yi Zhi, Yi Yin, famous cook), 14, 45, 48
*you* (presence), 20–21, 24, 137
Yu Zhengxie, 5
Yu, Pauline, 66–67, 123
Yuan, Haowen, 78
Yuan Hongdao, 83
Yuan Xingpei, 145n
Yuan Zongdao, 37, 82

Yuanwu, 35
*yuefu* (Music Department Songs), 121, 137, 155n
*yun* (tone), 107, 127, 137

Zeng Gong, 36, 138
Zeng Ji, 101, 138
Zhang Jian, 72
Zhang Longxi, 22–26, 67, 97
Zhang Wenxun, 91
Zhang Xian, 88–91, 138
Zhang Yan, 87–88
Zhang Zhu, 78–79
Zhao Nanxing, 82
Zhao Wen (zither master), 58, 138, 148n
*zhen di* (paramārtha-satya), 33–34, 138

Zheng Xie (Zheng Bangqiao), 85–87, 138
*zheng* (orthodoxy), 128, 138
*zhi* (intent), 32, 96, 124, 138
Zhong Ziqi (zither connoisseur), 117
Zhou Chi, 35
Zhou Zhenfu, 44
Zhu Guangqian, 91
Zhuang Zi (*Zhuang Zi*), 4–15, 22, 24–25, 28, 33–34, 41, 43, 46, 48, 54, 58, 60, 62, 68, 74–75, 78, 85, 104, 141n, 143n
Zigong (disciple of Confucius), 25, 138
Zilu (disciple of Confucius), 75, 138
Zu Baoquan, 67
*Zuo Zhuan*, 85, 138, 146n